Ethics: A Very Short Introduction

T0055143

VERY SHORT INTRODUCTIONS are for anyone wanting a stimulating and accessible way into a new subject. They are written by experts, and have been translated into more than 45 different languages.

The series began in 1995, and now covers a wide variety of topics in every discipline. The VSI library currently contains over 650 volumes—a Very Short Introduction to everything from Psychology and Philosophy of Science to American History and Relativity—and continues to grow in every subject area.

Very Short Introductions available now:

ABOLITIONISM Richard S. Newman
THE ABRAHAMIC RELIGIONS
   Charles L. Cohen
ACCOUNTING Christopher Nobes
ADAM SMITH Christopher J. Berry
ADOLESCENCE Peter K. Smith
ADVERTISING Winston Fletcher
AERIAL WARFARE Frank Ledwidge
AESTHETICS Bence Nanay
AFRICAN AMERICAN RELIGION
   Eddie S. Glaude Jr
AFRICAN HISTORY John Parker and
   Richard Rathbone
AFRICAN POLITICS Ian Taylor
AFRICAN RELIGIONS
   Jacob K. Olupona
AGEING Nancy A. Pachana
AGNOSTICISM Robin Le Poidevin
AGRICULTURE Paul Brassley and
   Richard Soffe
ALBERT CAMUS Oliver Gloag
ALEXANDER THE GREAT
   Hugh Bowden
ALGEBRA Peter M. Higgins
AMERICAN BUSINESS HISTORY
   Walter A. Friedman
AMERICAN CULTURAL HISTORY
   Eric Avila
AMERICAN FOREIGN RELATIONS
   Andrew Preston
AMERICAN HISTORY Paul S. Boyer
AMERICAN IMMIGRATION
   David A. Gerber
AMERICAN LEGAL HISTORY
   G. Edward White

AMERICAN MILITARY HISTORY
   Joseph T. Glatthaar
AMERICAN NAVAL
   HISTORY Craig L. Symonds
AMERICAN POLITICAL
   HISTORY Donald Critchlow
AMERICAN POLITICAL PARTIES
   AND ELECTIONS L. Sandy Maisel
AMERICAN POLITICS
   Richard M. Valelly
THE AMERICAN PRESIDENCY
   Charles O. Jones
THE AMERICAN REVOLUTION
   Robert J. Allison
AMERICAN SLAVERY
   Heather Andrea Williams
THE AMERICAN WEST Stephen Aron
AMERICAN WOMEN'S
   HISTORY Susan Ware
ANAESTHESIA Aidan O'Donnell
ANALYTIC PHILOSOPHY
   Michael Beaney
ANARCHISM Colin Ward
ANCIENT ASSYRIA Karen Radner
ANCIENT EGYPT Ian Shaw
ANCIENT EGYPTIAN ART AND
   ARCHITECTURE Christina Riggs
ANCIENT GREECE Paul Cartledge
THE ANCIENT NEAR EAST
   Amanda H. Podany
ANCIENT PHILOSOPHY Julia Annas
ANCIENT WARFARE Harry Sidebottom
ANGELS David Albert Jones
ANGLICANISM Mark Chapman
THE ANGLO-SAXON AGE John Blair

ANIMAL BEHAVIOUR
   Tristram D. Wyatt
THE ANIMAL KINGDOM
   Peter Holland
ANIMAL RIGHTS David DeGrazia
THE ANTARCTIC Klaus Dodds
ANTHROPOCENE Erle C. Ellis
ANTISEMITISM Steven Beller
ANXIETY Daniel Freeman and
   Jason Freeman
THE APOCRYPHAL GOSPELS
   Paul Foster
APPLIED MATHEMATICS
   Alain Goriely
ARCHAEOLOGY Paul Bahn
ARCHITECTURE Andrew Ballantyne
ARISTOCRACY William Doyle
ARISTOTLE Jonathan Barnes
ART HISTORY Dana Arnold
ART THEORY Cynthia Freeland
ARTIFICIAL INTELLIGENCE
   Margaret A. Boden
ASIAN AMERICAN HISTORY
   Madeline Y. Hsu
ASTROBIOLOGY David C. Catling
ASTROPHYSICS James Binney
ATHEISM Julian Baggini
THE ATMOSPHERE Paul I. Palmer
AUGUSTINE Henry Chadwick
AUSTRALIA Kenneth Morgan
AUTISM Uta Frith
AUTOBIOGRAPHY Laura Marcus
THE AVANT GARDE David Cottington
THE AZTECS David Carrasco
BABYLONIA Trevor Bryce
BACTERIA Sebastian G. B. Amyes
BANKING John Goddard and
   John O. S. Wilson
BARTHES Jonathan Culler
THE BEATS David Sterritt
BEAUTY Roger Scruton
BEHAVIOURAL ECONOMICS
   Michelle Baddeley
BESTSELLERS John Sutherland
THE BIBLE John Riches
BIBLICAL ARCHAEOLOGY
   Eric H. Cline
BIG DATA Dawn E. Holmes
BIOGEOGRAPHY Mark V. Lomolino
BIOGRAPHY Hermione Lee
BIOMETRICS Michael Fairhurst

BLACK HOLES Katherine Blundell
BLOOD Chris Cooper
THE BLUES Elijah Wald
THE BODY Chris Shilling
THE BOOK OF COMMON PRAYER
   Brian Cummings
THE BOOK OF MORMON
   Terryl Givens
BORDERS Alexander C. Diener and
   Joshua Hagen
THE BRAIN Michael O'Shea
BRANDING Robert Jones
THE BRICS Andrew F. Cooper
THE BRITISH CONSTITUTION
   Martin Loughlin
THE BRITISH EMPIRE Ashley Jackson
BRITISH POLITICS Tony Wright
BUDDHA Michael Carrithers
BUDDHISM Damien Keown
BUDDHIST ETHICS Damien Keown
BYZANTIUM Peter Sarris
C. S. LEWIS James Como
CALVINISM Jon Balserak
CANADA Donald Wright
CANCER Nicholas James
CAPITALISM James Fulcher
CATHOLICISM Gerald O'Collins
CAUSATION Stephen Mumford and
   Rani Lill Anjum
THE CELL Terence Allen and
   Graham Cowling
THE CELTS Barry Cunliffe
CHAOS Leonard Smith
CHARLES DICKENS Jenny Hartley
CHEMISTRY Peter Atkins
CHILD PSYCHOLOGY Usha Goswami
CHILDREN'S LITERATURE
   Kimberley Reynolds
CHINESE LITERATURE Sabina Knight
CHOICE THEORY Michael Allingham
CHRISTIAN ART Beth Williamson
CHRISTIAN ETHICS D. Stephen Long
CHRISTIANITY Linda Woodhead
CIRCADIAN RHYTHMS
   Russell Foster and Leon Kreitzman
CITIZENSHIP Richard Bellamy
CIVIL ENGINEERING
   David Muir Wood
CLASSICAL LITERATURE William Allan
CLASSICAL MYTHOLOGY
   Helen Morales

CLASSICS Mary Beard and
    John Henderson
CLAUSEWITZ Michael Howard
CLIMATE Mark Maslin
CLIMATE CHANGE Mark Maslin
CLINICAL PSYCHOLOGY
    Susan Llewelyn and
    Katie Aafjes-van Doorn
COGNITIVE NEUROSCIENCE
    Richard Passingham
THE COLD WAR Robert McMahon
COLONIAL AMERICA Alan Taylor
COLONIAL LATIN AMERICAN
    LITERATURE Rolena Adorno
COMBINATORICS Robin Wilson
COMEDY Matthew Bevis
COMMUNISM Leslie Holmes
COMPARATIVE LITERATURE
    Ben Hutchinson
COMPLEXITY John H. Holland
THE COMPUTER Darrel Ince
COMPUTER SCIENCE
    Subrata Dasgupta
CONCENTRATION CAMPS Dan Stone
CONFUCIANISM Daniel K. Gardner
THE CONQUISTADORS
    Matthew Restall and Felipe
    Fernández-Armesto
CONSCIENCE Paul Strohm
CONSCIOUSNESS Susan Blackmore
CONTEMPORARY ART
    Julian Stallabrass
CONTEMPORARY FICTION
    Robert Eaglestone
CONTINENTAL PHILOSOPHY
    Simon Critchley
COPERNICUS Owen Gingerich
CORAL REEFS Charles Sheppard
CORPORATE SOCIAL
    RESPONSIBILITY Jeremy Moon
CORRUPTION Leslie Holmes
COSMOLOGY Peter Coles
COUNTRY MUSIC Richard Carlin
CRIME FICTION Richard Bradford
CRIMINAL JUSTICE Julian V. Roberts
CRIMINOLOGY Tim Newburn
CRITICAL THEORY
    Stephen Eric Bronner
THE CRUSADES Christopher Tyerman
CRYPTOGRAPHY Fred Piper and
    Sean Murphy

CRYSTALLOGRAPHY A. M. Glazer
THE CULTURAL REVOLUTION
    Richard Curt Kraus
DADA AND SURREALISM
    David Hopkins
DANTE Peter Hainsworth and
    David Robey
DARWIN Jonathan Howard
THE DEAD SEA SCROLLS
    Timothy H. Lim
DECADENCE David Weir
DECOLONIZATION Dane Kennedy
DEMENTIA Kathleen Taylor
DEMOCRACY Bernard Crick
DEMOGRAPHY Sarah Harper
DEPRESSION Jan Scott and
    Mary Jane Tacchi
DERRIDA Simon Glendinning
DESCARTES Tom Sorell
DESERTS Nick Middleton
DESIGN John Heskett
DEVELOPMENT Ian Goldin
DEVELOPMENTAL BIOLOGY
    Lewis Wolpert
THE DEVIL Darren Oldridge
DIASPORA Kevin Kenny
DICTIONARIES Lynda Mugglestone
DINOSAURS David Norman
DIPLOMACY Joseph M. Siracusa
DOCUMENTARY FILM
    Patricia Aufderheide
DREAMING J. Allan Hobson
DRUGS Les Iversen
DRUIDS Barry Cunliffe
DYNASTY Jeroen Duindam
DYSLEXIA Margaret J. Snowling
EARLY MUSIC Thomas Forrest Kelly
THE EARTH Martin Redfern
EARTH SYSTEM SCIENCE Tim Lenton
ECOLOGY Jaboury Ghazoul
ECONOMICS Partha Dasgupta
EDUCATION Gary Thomas
EGYPTIAN MYTH Geraldine Pinch
EIGHTEENTH-CENTURY BRITAIN
    Paul Langford
THE ELEMENTS Philip Ball
ÉMILE ZOLA Brian Nelson
EMOTION Dylan Evans
EMPIRE Stephen Howe
ENERGY SYSTEMS Nick Jenkins
ENGELS Terrell Carver

ENGINEERING David Blockley
THE ENGLISH LANGUAGE
    Simon Horobin
ENGLISH LITERATURE Jonathan Bate
THE ENLIGHTENMENT
    John Robertson
ENTREPRENEURSHIP Paul Westhead
    and Mike Wright
ENVIRONMENTAL
    ECONOMICS Stephen Smith
ENVIRONMENTAL ETHICS
    Robin Attfield
ENVIRONMENTAL LAW
    Elizabeth Fisher
ENVIRONMENTAL POLITICS
    Andrew Dobson
ENZYMES Paul Engel
EPICUREANISM Catherine Wilson
EPIDEMIOLOGY Rodolfo Saracci
ETHICS Simon Blackburn
ETHNOMUSICOLOGY Timothy Rice
THE ETRUSCANS Christopher Smith
EUGENICS Philippa Levine
THE EUROPEAN UNION
    Simon Usherwood and John Pinder
EUROPEAN UNION LAW
    Anthony Arnull
EVOLUTION Brian and
    Deborah Charlesworth
EXISTENTIALISM Thomas Flynn
EXPLORATION Stewart A. Weaver
EXTINCTION Paul B. Wignall
THE EYE Michael Land
FAIRY TALE Marina Warner
FAMILY LAW Jonathan Herring
FASCISM Kevin Passmore
FASHION Rebecca Arnold
FEDERALISM Mark J. Rozell and
    Clyde Wilcox
FEMINISM Margaret Walters
FILM Michael Wood
FILM MUSIC Kathryn Kalinak
FILM NOIR James Naremore
FIRE Andrew C. Scott
THE FIRST WORLD WAR
    Michael Howard
FOLK MUSIC Mark Slobin
FOOD John Krebs
FORENSIC PSYCHOLOGY
    David Canter
FORENSIC SCIENCE Jim Fraser

FORESTS Jaboury Ghazoul
FOSSILS Keith Thomson
FOUCAULT Gary Gutting
THE FOUNDING FATHERS
    R. B. Bernstein
FRACTALS Kenneth Falconer
FREE SPEECH Nigel Warburton
FREE WILL Thomas Pink
FREEMASONRY Andreas Önnerfors
FRENCH LITERATURE John D. Lyons
FRENCH PHILOSOPHY
    Stephen Gaukroger and Knox Peden
THE FRENCH REVOLUTION
    William Doyle
FREUD Anthony Storr
FUNDAMENTALISM Malise Ruthven
FUNGI Nicholas P. Money
THE FUTURE Jennifer M. Gidley
GALAXIES John Gribbin
GALILEO Stillman Drake
GAME THEORY Ken Binmore
GANDHI Bhikhu Parekh
GARDEN HISTORY Gordon Campbell
GENES Jonathan Slack
GENIUS Andrew Robinson
GENOMICS John Archibald
GEOFFREY CHAUCER David Wallace
GEOGRAPHY John Matthews and
    David Herbert
GEOLOGY Jan Zalasiewicz
GEOPHYSICS William Lowrie
GEOPOLITICS Klaus Dodds
GEORGE BERNARD SHAW
    Christopher Wixson
GERMAN LITERATURE Nicholas Boyle
GERMAN PHILOSOPHY
    Andrew Bowie
THE GHETTO Bryan Cheyette
GLACIATION David J. A. Evans
GLOBAL CATASTROPHES Bill McGuire
GLOBAL ECONOMIC HISTORY
    Robert C. Allen
GLOBAL ISLAM Nile Green
GLOBALIZATION Manfred B. Steger
GOD John Bowker
GOETHE Ritchie Robertson
THE GOTHIC Nick Groom
GOVERNANCE Mark Bevir
GRAVITY Timothy Clifton
THE GREAT DEPRESSION AND THE
    NEW DEAL Eric Rauchway

HABERMAS James Gordon Finlayson
THE HABSBURG EMPIRE
    Martyn Rady
HAPPINESS Daniel M. Haybron
THE HARLEM RENAISSANCE
    Cheryl A. Wall
THE HEBREW BIBLE AS
    LITERATURE Tod Linafelt
HEGEL Peter Singer
HEIDEGGER Michael Inwood
THE HELLENISTIC AGE
    Peter Thonemann
HEREDITY John Waller
HERMENEUTICS Jens Zimmermann
HERODOTUS Jennifer T. Roberts
HIEROGLYPHS Penelope Wilson
HINDUISM Kim Knott
HISTORY John H. Arnold
THE HISTORY OF ASTRONOMY
    Michael Hoskin
THE HISTORY OF CHEMISTRY
    William H. Brock
THE HISTORY OF CHILDHOOD
    James Marten
THE HISTORY OF CINEMA
    Geoffrey Nowell-Smith
THE HISTORY OF LIFE
    Michael Benton
THE HISTORY OF MATHEMATICS
    Jacqueline Stedall
THE HISTORY OF MEDICINE
    William Bynum
THE HISTORY OF PHYSICS
    J. L. Heilbron
THE HISTORY OF TIME
    Leofranc Holford-Strevens
HIV AND AIDS Alan Whiteside
HOBBES Richard Tuck
HOLLYWOOD Peter Decherney
THE HOLY ROMAN EMPIRE
    Joachim Whaley
HOME Michael Allen Fox
HOMER Barbara Graziosi
HORMONES Martin Luck
HUMAN ANATOMY
    Leslie Klenerman
HUMAN EVOLUTION Bernard Wood
HUMAN RIGHTS Andrew Clapham
HUMANISM Stephen Law
HUME A. J. Ayer

HUMOUR Noël Carroll
THE ICE AGE Jamie Woodward
IDENTITY Florian Coulmas
IDEOLOGY Michael Freeden
THE IMMUNE SYSTEM
    Paul Klenerman
INDIAN CINEMA Ashish Rajadhyaksha
INDIAN PHILOSOPHY Sue Hamilton
THE INDUSTRIAL REVOLUTION
    Robert C. Allen
INFECTIOUS DISEASE Marta L. Wayne
    and Benjamin M. Bolker
INFINITY Ian Stewart
INFORMATION Luciano Floridi
INNOVATION Mark Dodgson and
    David Gann
INTELLECTUAL PROPERTY
    Siva Vaidhyanathan
INTELLIGENCE Ian J. Deary
INTERNATIONAL LAW
    Vaughan Lowe
INTERNATIONAL MIGRATION
    Khalid Koser
INTERNATIONAL RELATIONS
    Christian Reus-Smit
INTERNATIONAL SECURITY
    Christopher S. Browning
IRAN Ali M. Ansari
ISLAM Malise Ruthven
ISLAMIC HISTORY Adam Silverstein
ISLAMIC LAW Mashood A. Baderin
ISOTOPES Rob Ellam
ITALIAN LITERATURE
    Peter Hainsworth and David Robey
JESUS Richard Bauckham
JEWISH HISTORY David N. Myers
JOURNALISM Ian Hargreaves
JUDAISM Norman Solomon
JUNG Anthony Stevens
KABBALAH Joseph Dan
KAFKA Ritchie Robertson
KANT Roger Scruton
KEYNES Robert Skidelsky
KIERKEGAARD Patrick Gardiner
KNOWLEDGE Jennifer Nagel
THE KORAN Michael Cook
KOREA Michael J. Seth
LAKES Warwick F. Vincent
LANDSCAPE ARCHITECTURE
    Ian H. Thompson

LANDSCAPES AND
    GEOMORPHOLOGY
    Andrew Goudie and Heather Viles
LANGUAGES Stephen R. Anderson
LATE ANTIQUITY Gillian Clark
LAW Raymond Wacks
THE LAWS OF THERMODYNAMICS
    Peter Atkins
LEADERSHIP Keith Grint
LEARNING Mark Haselgrove
LEIBNIZ Maria Rosa Antognazza
LEO TOLSTOY Liza Knapp
LIBERALISM Michael Freeden
LIGHT Ian Walmsley
LINCOLN Allen C. Guelzo
LINGUISTICS Peter Matthews
LITERARY THEORY Jonathan Culler
LOCKE John Dunn
LOGIC Graham Priest
LOVE Ronald de Sousa
MACHIAVELLI Quentin Skinner
MADNESS Andrew Scull
MAGIC Owen Davies
MAGNA CARTA Nicholas Vincent
MAGNETISM Stephen Blundell
MALTHUS Donald Winch
MAMMALS T. S. Kemp
MANAGEMENT John Hendry
MAO Delia Davin
MARINE BIOLOGY Philip V. Mladenov
MARKETING
    Kenneth Le Meunier-FitzHugh
THE MARQUIS DE SADE
    John Phillips
MARTIN LUTHER Scott H. Hendrix
MARTYRDOM Jolyon Mitchell
MARX Peter Singer
MATERIALS Christopher Hall
MATHEMATICAL FINANCE
    Mark H. A. Davis
MATHEMATICS Timothy Gowers
MATTER Geoff Cottrell
THE MAYA Matthew Restall and
    Amara Solari
THE MEANING OF LIFE
    Terry Eagleton
MEASUREMENT David Hand
MEDICAL ETHICS Michael Dunn and
    Tony Hope
MEDICAL LAW Charles Foster

MEDIEVAL BRITAIN John Gillingham
    and Ralph A. Griffiths
MEDIEVAL LITERATURE
    Elaine Treharne
MEDIEVAL PHILOSOPHY
    John Marenbon
MEMORY Jonathan K. Foster
METAPHYSICS Stephen Mumford
METHODISM William J. Abraham
THE MEXICAN
    REVOLUTION Alan Knight
MICHAEL FARADAY
    Frank A. J. L. James
MICROBIOLOGY Nicholas P. Money
MICROECONOMICS Avinash Dixit
MICROSCOPY Terence Allen
THE MIDDLE AGES Miri Rubin
MILITARY JUSTICE Eugene R. Fidell
MILITARY STRATEGY
    Antulio J. Echevarria II
MINERALS David Vaughan
MIRACLES Yujin Nagasawa
MODERN ARCHITECTURE
    Adam Sharr
MODERN ART David Cottington
MODERN CHINA Rana Mitter
MODERN DRAMA
    Kirsten E. Shepherd-Barr
MODERN FRANCE
    Vanessa R. Schwartz
MODERN INDIA Craig Jeffrey
MODERN IRELAND Senia Pašeta
MODERN ITALY Anna Cento Bull
MODERN JAPAN
    Christopher Goto-Jones
MODERN LATIN AMERICAN
    LITERATURE
    Roberto González Echevarría
MODERN WAR Richard English
MODERNISM Christopher Butler
MOLECULAR BIOLOGY Aysha Divan
    and Janice A. Royds
MOLECULES Philip Ball
MONASTICISM Stephen J. Davis
THE MONGOLS Morris Rossabi
MONTAIGNE William M. Hamlin
MOONS David A. Rothery
MORMONISM Richard Lyman Bushman
MOUNTAINS Martin F. Price
MUHAMMAD Jonathan A. C. Brown

MULTICULTURALISM Ali Rattansi
MULTILINGUALISM John C. Maher
MUSIC Nicholas Cook
MYTH Robert A. Segal
NAPOLEON David Bell
THE NAPOLEONIC WARS
Mike Rapport
NATIONALISM Steven Grosby
NATIVE AMERICAN
LITERATURE Sean Teuton
NAVIGATION Jim Bennett
NAZI GERMANY Jane Caplan
NELSON MANDELA Elleke Boehmer
NEOLIBERALISM Manfred B. Steger
and Ravi K. Roy
NETWORKS Guido Caldarelli and
Michele Catanzaro
THE NEW TESTAMENT
Luke Timothy Johnson
THE NEW TESTAMENT AS
LITERATURE Kyle Keefer
NEWTON Robert Iliffe
NIELS BOHR J. L. Heilbron
NIETZSCHE Michael Tanner
NINETEENTH-CENTURY
BRITAIN Christopher Harvie and
H. C. G. Matthew
THE NORMAN CONQUEST
George Garnett
NORTH AMERICAN INDIANS
Theda Perdue and Michael D. Green
NORTHERN IRELAND
Marc Mulholland
NOTHING Frank Close
NUCLEAR PHYSICS Frank Close
NUCLEAR POWER Maxwell Irvine
NUCLEAR
WEAPONS Joseph M. Siracusa
NUMBER THEORY Robin Wilson
NUMBERS Peter M. Higgins
NUTRITION David A. Bender
OBJECTIVITY Stephen Gaukroger
OCEANS Dorrik Stow
THE OLD TESTAMENT
Michael D. Coogan
THE ORCHESTRA D. Kern Holoman
ORGANIC CHEMISTRY
Graham Patrick
ORGANIZATIONS Mary Jo Hatch

ORGANIZED CRIME
Georgios A. Antonopoulos and
Georgios Papanicolaou
ORTHODOX CHRISTIANITY
A. Edward Siecienski
OVID Llewelyn Morgan
PAGANISM Owen Davies
PAIN Rob Boddice
THE PALESTINIAN-ISRAELI
CONFLICT Martin Bunton
PANDEMICS Christian W. McMillen
PARTICLE PHYSICS Frank Close
PAUL E. P. Sanders
PEACE Oliver P. Richmond
PENTECOSTALISM William K. Kay
PERCEPTION Brian Rogers
THE PERIODIC TABLE Eric R. Scerri
PHILOSOPHICAL METHOD
Timothy Williamson
PHILOSOPHY Edward Craig
PHILOSOPHY IN THE ISLAMIC
WORLD Peter Adamson
PHILOSOPHY OF BIOLOGY
Samir Okasha
PHILOSOPHY OF LAW
Raymond Wacks
PHILOSOPHY OF SCIENCE
Samir Okasha
PHILOSOPHY OF
RELIGION Tim Bayne
PHOTOGRAPHY Steve Edwards
PHYSICAL CHEMISTRY Peter Atkins
PHYSICS Sidney Perkowitz
PILGRIMAGE Ian Reader
PLAGUE Paul Slack
PLANETS David A. Rothery
PLANTS Timothy Walker
PLATE TECTONICS Peter Molnar
PLATO Julia Annas
POETRY Bernard O'Donoghue
POLITICAL PHILOSOPHY David Miller
POLITICS Kenneth Minogue
POPULISM Cas Mudde and Cristóbal
Rovira Kaltwasser
POSTCOLONIALISM Robert Young
POSTMODERNISM
Christopher Butler
POSTSTRUCTURALISM
Catherine Belsey

POVERTY Philip N. Jefferson
PREHISTORY Chris Gosden
PRESOCRATIC PHILOSOPHY
    Catherine Osborne
PRIVACY Raymond Wacks
PROBABILITY John Haigh
PROGRESSIVISM Walter Nugent
PROHIBITION W. J. Rorabaugh
PROJECTS Andrew Davies
PROTESTANTISM Mark A. Noll
PSYCHIATRY Tom Burns
PSYCHOANALYSIS Daniel Pick
PSYCHOLOGY Gillian Butler and
    Freda McManus
PSYCHOLOGY OF MUSIC
    Elizabeth Hellmuth Margulis
PSYCHOPATHY Essi Viding
PSYCHOTHERAPY Tom Burns and
    Eva Burns-Lundgren
PUBLIC ADMINISTRATION
    Stella Z. Theodoulou and Ravi K. Roy
PUBLIC HEALTH Virginia Berridge
PURITANISM Francis J. Bremer
THE QUAKERS Pink Dandelion
QUANTUM THEORY
    John Polkinghorne
RACISM Ali Rattansi
RADIOACTIVITY Claudio Tuniz
RASTAFARI Ennis B. Edmonds
READING Belinda Jack
THE REAGAN REVOLUTION Gil Troy
REALITY Jan Westerhoff
RECONSTRUCTION Allen C. Guelzo
THE REFORMATION Peter Marshall
RELATIVITY Russell Stannard
RELIGION Thomas A. Tweed
RELIGION IN AMERICA Timothy Beal
THE RENAISSANCE Jerry Brotton
RENAISSANCE ART
    Geraldine A. Johnson
RENEWABLE ENERGY Nick Jelley
REPTILES T. S. Kemp
REVOLUTIONS Jack A. Goldstone
RHETORIC Richard Toye
RISK Baruch Fischhoff and John Kadvany
RITUAL Barry Stephenson
RIVERS Nick Middleton
ROBOTICS Alan Winfield
ROCKS Jan Zalasiewicz

ROMAN BRITAIN Peter Salway
THE ROMAN EMPIRE
    Christopher Kelly
THE ROMAN REPUBLIC
    David M. Gwynn
ROMANTICISM Michael Ferber
ROUSSEAU Robert Wokler
RUSSELL A. C. Grayling
THE RUSSIAN ECONOMY
    Richard Connolly
RUSSIAN HISTORY Geoffrey Hosking
RUSSIAN LITERATURE Catriona Kelly
THE RUSSIAN REVOLUTION
    S. A. Smith
SAINTS Simon Yarrow
SAVANNAS Peter A. Furley
SCEPTICISM Duncan Pritchard
SCHIZOPHRENIA Chris Frith and
    Eve Johnstone
SCHOPENHAUER Christopher Janaway
SCIENCE AND RELIGION
    Thomas Dixon
SCIENCE FICTION David Seed
THE SCIENTIFIC REVOLUTION
    Lawrence M. Principe
SCOTLAND Rab Houston
SECULARISM Andrew Copson
SEXUAL SELECTION Marlene Zuk and
    Leigh W. Simmons
SEXUALITY Véronique Mottier
SHAKESPEARE'S COMEDIES
    Bart van Es
SHAKESPEARE'S SONNETS AND
    POEMS Jonathan F. S. Post
SHAKESPEARE'S TRAGEDIES
    Stanley Wells
SIKHISM Eleanor Nesbitt
THE SILK ROAD James A. Millward
SLANG Jonathon Green
SLEEP Steven W. Lockley and
    Russell G. Foster
SMELL Matthew Cobb
SOCIAL AND CULTURAL
    ANTHROPOLOGY
    John Monaghan and Peter Just
SOCIAL PSYCHOLOGY
    Richard J. Crisp
SOCIAL WORK Sally Holland and
    Jonathan Scourfield

SOCIALISM Michael Newman
SOCIOLINGUISTICS John Edwards
SOCIOLOGY Steve Bruce
SOCRATES C. C. W. Taylor
SOFT MATTER Tom McLeish
SOUND Mike Goldsmith
SOUTHEAST ASIA James R. Rush
THE SOVIET UNION Stephen Lovell
THE SPANISH CIVIL WAR
   Helen Graham
SPANISH LITERATURE Jo Labanyi
SPINOZA Roger Scruton
SPIRITUALITY Philip Sheldrake
SPORT Mike Cronin
STARS Andrew King
STATISTICS David J. Hand
STEM CELLS Jonathan Slack
STOICISM Brad Inwood
STRUCTURAL ENGINEERING
   David Blockley
STUART BRITAIN John Morrill
THE SUN Philip Judge
SUPERCONDUCTIVITY
   Stephen Blundell
SUPERSTITION Stuart Vyse
SYMMETRY Ian Stewart
SYNAESTHESIA Julia Simner
SYNTHETIC BIOLOGY Jamie A. Davies
SYSTEMS BIOLOGY Eberhard O. Voit
TAXATION Stephen Smith
TEETH Peter S. Ungar
TELESCOPES Geoff Cottrell
TERRORISM Charles Townshend
THEATRE Marvin Carlson
THEOLOGY David F. Ford
THINKING AND REASONING
   Jonathan St B. T. Evans
THOMAS AQUINAS Fergus Kerr
THOUGHT Tim Bayne
TIBETAN BUDDHISM
   Matthew T. Kapstein
TIDES David George Bowers and
   Emyr Martyn Roberts
TOCQUEVILLE Harvey C. Mansfield
TOPOLOGY Richard Earl
TRAGEDY Adrian Poole
TRANSLATION Matthew Reynolds
THE TREATY OF VERSAILLES
   Michael S. Neiberg
TRIGONOMETRY
   Glen Van Brummelen
THE TROJAN WAR Eric H. Cline
TRUST Katherine Hawley
THE TUDORS John Guy
TWENTIETH-CENTURY BRITAIN
   Kenneth O. Morgan
TYPOGRAPHY Paul Luna
THE UNITED NATIONS
   Jussi M. Hanhimäki
UNIVERSITIES AND COLLEGES
   David Palfreyman and Paul Temple
THE U.S. CIVIL WAR
   Louis P. Masur
THE U.S. CONGRESS Donald A. Ritchie
THE U.S. CONSTITUTION
   David J. Bodenhamer
THE U.S. SUPREME COURT
   Linda Greenhouse
UTILITARIANISM Katarzyna de
   Lazari-Radek and Peter Singer
UTOPIANISM Lyman Tower Sargent
VETERINARY SCIENCE James Yeates
THE VIKINGS Julian D. Richards
VIRUSES Dorothy H. Crawford
VOLCANOES Michael J. Branney and
   Jan Zalasiewicz
VOLTAIRE Nicholas Cronk
WAR AND TECHNOLOGY Alex Roland
WATER John Finney
WAVES Mike Goldsmith
WEATHER Storm Dunlop
THE WELFARE STATE David Garland
WILLIAM SHAKESPEARE
   Stanley Wells
WITCHCRAFT Malcolm Gaskill
WITTGENSTEIN A. C. Grayling
WORK Stephen Fineman
WORLD MUSIC Philip Bohlman
THE WORLD TRADE
   ORGANIZATION Amrita Narlikar
WORLD WAR II Gerhard L. Weinberg
WRITING AND SCRIPT
   Andrew Robinson
ZIONISM Michael Stanislawski

Simon Blackburn

ETHICS

A Very Short Introduction

SECOND EDITION

OXFORD
UNIVERSITY PRESS

Great Clarendon Street, Oxford, OX2 6DP,
United Kingdom

Oxford University Press is a department of the University of Oxford.
It furthers the University's objective of excellence in research, scholarship,
and education by publishing worldwide. Oxford is a registered trade mark of
Oxford University Press in the UK and in certain other countries

© Simon Blackburn 2021

The moral rights of the author have been asserted

First published as an Oxford University Press Hardback 2001
First published as an Oxford University Press Paperback 2002
First published as a Very Short Introduction 2003
This edition published 2021

Published in the United States of America by Oxford University Press
198 Madison Avenue, New York, NY 10016, United States of America

British Library Cataloguing in Publication Data
Data available

Library of Congress Control Number: 2020945713

ISBN 978-0-19-886810-1

Printed and bound by CPI Group (UK) Ltd, Croydon, CR0 4YY

Contents

Preface to second edition xvii

Introduction 1

1 Seven threats to thinking about ethics 7

2 Foundations 40

3 Some ethical ideas 66

References 99

Further reading 103

Index 105

Preface to second edition

In the Preface to the first edition of this book I described how
I had felt motivated to write it by the fear that most introductions
to ethics fail to engage with what really bothers people about the
subject. What really bothers them, I felt, was the fear that ethical
thought and ethical claims are really a kind of sham. So I
structured the work as a response to some of those fears.

That edition was published in 2001. Since then times have
changed. We live in a less optimistic world. We are also more
aware of disasters in our moral and political environment.
Virtually everywhere politics is conducted more angrily, but also
more independently of truth or reason. In 2001 I could write that
the moral climate is largely invisible to people; now that is not so.
Toleration has noticeably increased in some areas, such as
the acceptance of gay and transgendered people (and lying
politicians), but decreased in others. Free speech is often under
threat, while people everywhere seem happy to take advantage of
the relative immunity of the web to moralize and blame and
shame other people. More conduct is out of bounds, sometimes as
it should be, but it is widely feared that cooperation, trust, and
trustworthiness have declined. So it is a good time to revisit ethics
and how to think about it and its place in our lives.

The first edition was written while I was still in post as a teacher, and I thanked the wonderful Research School of Social Sciences at the Australian National University for the interlude it gave me in which the book was written. Now that I am retired from full-time teaching I have to thank Trinity College, Cambridge, for the generous support it offers to elderly Fellows. And, just as before, I wish to thank my wife for putting her editorial skills at my disposal, for her forbearance, and for her unfailing patience and good cheer.

Introduction

An ethical environment is the surrounding climate of ideas about how to live. It determines what we find acceptable, or unacceptable, admirable or contemptible. It determines our conception of when things are going well and when they are going badly. It determines our conception of what is due to us, and what is due from us, as we relate to others. It shapes our emotional responses, determining what is a cause of pride or shame, or anger or gratitude, or what can be forgiven and what cannot. It gives us our standards—our standards of behaviour. In the eyes of some thinkers, most famously perhaps G. W. F. Hegel (1770–1831), it shapes our very identities. Our consciousness of ourselves is largely or even essentially a consciousness of how we stand for other people. We need stories of our own value in the eyes of each other, the eyes of the world.

We are apt to take our own ideas for granted, so much so that we may not even be aware of them. It is as if they form the lens through which we see the social world, but we may not be aware of the lenses themselves. Our ethical ideas are manifested in our tendencies to accept or reject routes of thought and feeling, and we may not recognize these in ourselves, or even be able to articulate them. Yet such tendencies make up the ethical climate that surrounds us, and they rule the social and political world.

An *ethical* climate is a very different thing from a *moralistic* one. Indeed, one of the marks of an ethical climate may be hostility to moralizing, which may be out of place or bad form. Thinking that will itself be a disposition affecting the way we live our lives. So, for instance, one peculiarity of our present climate is that we care much more about our rights than about our 'good'. For many ethical traditions across the world the central concern was the state of one's soul, meaning some personal state of piety, justice, or harmony. Such a state might include resignation and renunciation, or detachment or obedience or knowledge, especially self-knowledge. For Plato there could be no just political order except one populated by just citizens, although this also allows that inner harmony or 'justice' in citizens requires a just political order—there is nothing viciously circular about this interplay. Chickens and eggs have evolved together. (But we should reflect they might also go extinct together, as can justice and honesty in citizens and justice and honesty in our political state.)

Today we tend not to care so much about the state of our souls: we tend to think that modern constitutional democracies are fine regardless of the private vices of those within them. We are much more nervous talking about our good: it seems moralistic, or undemocratic or elitist. Similarly, we are nervous talking about duty. The Victorian ideal of a life devoted to duty, or a calling, is substantially lost to us. So a greater proportion of our moral energy goes to protecting claims against each other, and that includes protecting the state of our soul as purely private, purely our own business. We have a right, we think, to be as we are. We assert that we have a right to our own opinions, however stupid or careless we apparently were in forming them. We see some of the workings of this aspect of our climate in this book.

Human beings are ethical animals. I do not mean that we naturally behave particularly well, nor that we are endlessly telling each other what to do. But we grade and evaluate, and compare and admire, and claim and justify. We do not just 'prefer' this or that, in isolation. We prefer that our preferences are shared; when they are important to us we turn them into demands on each other. Events endlessly adjust our sense of responsibility, our guilt and shame and our sense of our own worth and that of others. We hope for lives whose story leaves us looking admirable; we like our weaknesses to be hidden and deniable. Drama, literature, and poetry all work out ideas of standards of behaviour and their consequences. This is overtly so in great art. But it shows itself just as unmistakably in the unfortunate prevalence of gossip and the popularity of confession shows and soap operas.

Reflection on the ethical climate is not the private preserve of a few academic theorists in universities. The satirist and cartoonist, as well as the artist and the novelist, comment upon and criticize the prevailing climate just as effectively as those who get known as philosophers. The impact of a campaigning novelist, such as Harriet Beecher Stowe, Dickens, Zola, or Solzhenitzyn, may be much greater than that of the academic theorist. A single photograph may have done more to halt the Vietnam war than all the writings of moral philosophers of the time put together.

Philosophy is certainly not alone in its engagement with the ethical climate. But its reflections contain a distinctive ambition. The ambition is to understand the springs of motivation, reason, and feeling that move us. It is to understand the networks of rules or 'norms' that sustain our lives. The ambition is often one of finding system in the apparent jumble of principles and goals that we respect, or say we do, although some philosophers take a different tack, and tell us not only to put up with the jumble, but to celebrate it. Either way, it involves the hope of increased self-knowledge. Of course, philosophers do not escape the climate, even as they reflect on it. Any story about human nature in the contemporary climate is a result of human nature and the contemporary climate. But such stories may be better or worse, for all that.

Admiring the enterprise, aspiring to it, and even tolerating it, are themselves moral stances. They can themselves flourish or wither at different times, depending on how much we like what we see in the mirror. Rejecting the enterprise is natural enough, especially when things are comfortable. After all, we do not like being told what to do, and become especially defensive when we are bent on behaving badly. We want to enjoy our lives, and we want to enjoy them with a good conscience. People who disturb that equilibrium are uncomfortable, so moralists and critics are often uninvited guests at the feast, and we have a multitude of defences against them. Analogously, some individuals can insulate themselves from a poor physical environment, for a time. They may profit by creating one. The owner can live upwind of his chemical factory, and the logger may know that the trees will not give out until after he is dead. Similarly, individuals can insulate themselves from a poor moral environment, or profit from it. Just as weeds flourish at the expense of other plants, so do some people. Those of us who do not like a fight can be exploited by others. The litter lout or the fly-tipper gets away with it because most observers would be frightened of intervening, while to as much as toot your horn at another motorist can risk a trip to hospital.

Ethics is disturbing. We are often vaguely uncomfortable when we think of such things as exploitation of the world's resources, or the way our comforts are provided by the miserable labour conditions of the third world. Sometimes, defensively, we get angry when such things are brought up. But to be entrenched in a culture, rather than merely belonging to the occasional rogue, exploitative attitudes will themselves need a story. So an ethical climate may allow talking of 'the market' as a justification for *our* high prices, and talking of 'their selfishness' and 'our rights' as a justification for anger at *their* high prices. Racists and sexists, like antebellum slave owners in America, always have to tell themselves a story that justifies their system. The ethical climate will sustain a conviction that *we* are civilized, and *they* are not, or that *we* deserve our better fortune more than *them*, or that *we* are

4

intelligent, sensitive, rational, or progressive, or scientific, or authoritative, or blessed, or alone are to be trusted with freedoms and rights, while *they* are not. An ethic gone wrong is an essential preliminary to the sweat-shop, or the concentration camp and the death march.

I therefore begin this book with a look at the responses we sometimes give when ethics intrudes on our lives. These are responses that in different ways constitute threats to ethical thinking. After that, in Part 2, we look at the question of foundations: the ultimate justification for ethics, and its connection with human knowledge and human progress. Finally, in Part 3 we look at some of the problems that living throws at us, using some of the materials of the first two parts.

Part 1
Seven threats to thinking about ethics

This part does not look at the threat to ethical behaviour arising from the sins and weaknesses that make us behave badly. I only visit these depressing sources of some of the ills of the world at the end of the book. This part looks instead at ideas that destabilize us when we think about standards of choice and conduct. In various ways these ideas seem to suggest that ethical thought is somehow impossible. They are important because they themselves can seep into the moral environment. When they do, they can change what we expect from each other and ourselves, usually for the worse. After that happens, when we look at the big words—justice, equality, freedom, rights—we are likely to see only bids for power and clashes of power, or we see only hypocrisy, or we see only our own opinions, unworthy to be foisted onto others. Scepticism, cynicism, and self-consciousness threaten to paralyse us. In this part we look at seven such threats.

1. The threat of the death of God

For many people, ethics is not only tied up with religion, but is completely settled by it. Such people do not need to think too much about ethics, because there is an authoritative code of instructions, a handbook of how to live. It is the word of Heaven, or the will of a Being greater than ourselves. The standards of living become known to us by revelation of this Being. Either we take ourselves to perceive the fountainhead directly, or more often we have the benefit of an intermediary—a priest, or a prophet, a text, or a tradition sufficiently in touch with the divine will to be able to communicate it to us. Then we know what to do. Obedience to the divine will is meritorious, and brings reward; disobedience is lethally punished. In the Christian version, obedience brings triumph over death, or everlasting life. Disobedience means eternal Hell.

In the 19th century, in the West, when traditional religious belief began to lose its grip, many thinkers felt that ethics went with it. It is not to the purpose here to assess whether such belief should have lost its grip. Our question is the implication for our standards of behaviour. Is it true that, as Dostoevsky said, 'If God is dead, everything is permitted'? It might seem to be true: without a lawgiver, how can there be a law?

Before thinking about this more directly, we might take a diversion through some of the shortcomings in traditional religious instruction. Anyone reading the Bible might be troubled by some of its precepts. The Old Testament God is partial to some people above others, and above all jealous of his own pre-eminence, a strange moral obsession. He seems to have no problem with a slave-owning society (Exodus 21: 7 explains how slavery of daughters should be conducted), believes that birth control is a capital crime (Genesis 38: 9–10), is keen on child abuse (Proverbs 22: 15, 23: 13, 23: 14, 26: 3), and for good measure, approves of fool abuse (Prov. 29: 15).

Things are usually supposed to get better in the New Testament, with its admirable emphasis on love, forgiveness, and meekness. Yet the overall story of 'atonement' and 'redemption' is morally dubious, suggesting as it does that justice can be satisfied by the sacrifice of an innocent for the sins of the guilty—the doctrine of the scapegoat. Then the persona of Jesus in the Gospels has his fair share of moral quirks. He can be sectarian: 'Go not into the

8

way of the gentiles, and into any city of the Samaritans enter ye not. But go rather to the lost sheep of the House of Israel' (Matthew 10: 5–6). In a similar vein, he dismisses the non-Jewish woman from Canaan who had asked for help with the chilling racist remark: 'It is not meet to take the children's bread and cast it to dogs' (Matt. 15: 26). He wants us to be gentle, meek, and mild, but he himself is far from it: 'Ye serpents, ye generation of vipers, how can ye escape the damnation of Hell?' (Matt. 23: 33). The episode of the Gadarene swine shows him to share the then-popular belief that mental illness is caused by possession by devils. It also shows that animal lives—also anybody else's property rights in pigs—have no value (Matt. 17: 15–21, Luke 8: 28–33). The events of the fig tree in Bethany (Mark 11:12–21) would make any environmentalist's hair stand on end.

Finally there are sins of omission as well as sins of commission. So we might wonder as well why he is not shown explicitly countermanding some of the rough bits of the Old Testament. Exodus 22: 18, 'Thou shalt not suffer a witch to live', helped to burn alive tens or hundreds of thousands of women in Europe and America, between around 1450 and 1780. It would have been helpful to suffering humanity, one might think, had a supremely good and caring and knowledgeable God, foreseeing this, revoked the injunction.

All in all then the Bible can be read as giving us a carte blanche for harsh attitudes to children, the mentally handicapped, animals, the environment, the divorced, unbelievers, people with various sexual habits, and elderly women. It encourages harsh attitudes to ourselves, as fallen creatures, endlessly polluted by sin, and hatred of ourselves inevitably brings hatred of others.

Obviously there have been, and will be, apologists who want to defend or explain away the embarrassing elements. Similarly, apologists for Hinduism defend or explain away its involvement with the caste system, and apologists for Islam defend or explain away its harsh penal code, its attitudes to women, and its alarming tendency to put to death people of other faiths or no faith, and especially people who lose their faith in Islam. What is interesting however is that when we weigh up these attempts we are ourselves in the process of assessing moral standards. We are able to stand far enough back from any text or tradition, however entrenched, to ask whether it represents an admirable or acceptable morality, or whether we ought to accept some bits, but reject others.

The classic challenge to the idea that ethics either needs or can be given a religious foundation is provided in Plato, in the dialogue known as *The Euthyphro*. In this dialogue, Socrates, who is on the point of being tried for impiety, encounters one Euthyphro, who sets himself up as knowing exactly what piety or justice is. Indeed, he is so sure of this that he is on the point of prosecuting his own father for causing a death. Socrates challenges him by asking: 'The point which I should first wish to understand is whether the pious or holy is beloved by the gods because it is holy, or holy because it is beloved of the gods.' Once he has posed this question, Socrates has no trouble coming down on one side of it:

> 'I mean to say that the holy has been acknowledged by us to be loved of God because it is holy, not to be holy because it is loved.'

The point is that God, or the gods, are not to be thought of as *arbitrary*. They have to be regarded as selecting the *right* things to allow and to forbid. *They* have to latch on to what is holy or just, exactly as we do. It is not given that they do this simply because they are powerful, or created everything, or have horrendous punishments and delicious rewards in their gifts. That doesn't make them *good*. Furthermore, to obey their commandments just because of their power would be servile and self-interested. Suppose, for instance, I am minded to do something bad, such as to betray someone's trust. It isn't good enough if I think, 'Well, let me see, the gains are such-and-such, but now I have to factor in the chance of God hitting me hard if I do it. On the other hand,

God is forgiving and there is a good chance I can fob him off by confession, or by a deathbed repentance later...' These are not the thoughts of a good character. The good character is supposed to think, 'It would be a betrayal, so I won't do it.' That's the end of the story. To go in for a religious cost–benefit analysis is, in a phrase made famous by the contemporary moral philosopher Bernard Williams, to have 'one thought too many'.

The detour through an external god, then, seems worse than irrelevant. It seems to distort the very idea of a standard of conduct. As the moral philosopher Immanuel Kant put it, it encourages us to act in *accordance* with a rule, but only because of fear of punishment or some other incentive. Whereas what we really want is for people to act out of *respect* for a rule. This is what true virtue requires (I discuss these ideas of Kant more fully in Part 2).

We might wonder whether only a vulgarized religion is a target for this kind of critique. The question then becomes, what other kind is there? A more adequate conception of God should certainly stop him from being a vindictive old man in the sky. Something more abstract, perhaps? But in that mystical direction lies a god who stands a long way away from human beings, and also from human good or bad. As the Greek Epicurus (341–271 BC) put it:

> The blessed and immortal nature knows no trouble itself nor causes trouble to any other, so that it is never constrained by anger or favour. For all such things exist only in the weak.

A really blessed and immortal nature is simply too *grand* to be bothered by the doings of tiny human beings. It would be unfitting for it to be worked up over whether human beings eat shellfish, or have sex one way or another.

The alternative suggested by Plato's dialogue is that religion gives a mythical clothing and mythical authority to a morality that is

11

just there to begin with. Myth, in this sense, is not to be despised. It gives us symbolism and examples that engage our imaginations. It is the depository for humanity's endless attempts to struggle with death, desire, happiness, and good and evil. When an exile reminisces, she will remember the songs and poems and folktales of the homeland rather than its laws or its constitution. If the songs no longer speak to her, she is on the way to forgetting. Similarly, we may fear that when religion no longer speaks to us, we may be on our way to forgetting some important part of history and human experience. This may be a moral change, for better or worse. In this analysis, religion is not the foundation of ethics, but its showcase or its symbolic expression. It provides the music and the poetry with which ethics is displayed.

But it is more than that, for we drape our own standards with the stories of divine origin as a way of cementing their authority. We do not *just* have a standard of conduct that forbids, say, murder, but we have mythological historical examples in which God expressed his displeasure at cases of murder. Unhappily myth and religion stand at the service of bad morals as well. We read back what we put in, magnified and validated. We do not just fear science, or want to take other people's land, but we have examples in which God punishes the desire for knowledge, or commands us to occupy the territory. We have God's authority for dominating women, or children, or nature, and for regarding *them*—others different from ourselves—as inferior, or even criminal. In other words, we have the full depressing spectacle of people not only wanting to do something, but projecting upon their gods the commands making it a right or even a duty to do it. The prisons containing convicted terrorists are filled with deluded young men convinced that their holy book has told them that almost everyone else must be killed.

Religion on this account is not the source of standards of behaviour, but a projection of them, made precisely in order to dress them up with an absolute authority. Religion serves to keep *us* apart from *them*, and no doubt it has other social and psychological functions as well. It can certainly be the means whereby unjust political authority keeps its subjects docile. The words of the hymn—God made the rich man in his castle and the poor man at his gate—help to keep the lower orders resigned to their fates. It's good for the bosses, but it is also some good for the underdogs, for it can be, as Marx famously put it, the opium of the people, giving them a narcotic consolation for existence in a harsh social world. Finally, as the sociologist Émile Durkheim emphasized, the very arbitrariness of religious practices—the rules determining what is sacred and what is not, what to eat, how to dress, how rituals are to be performed, and so on—serve further to separate *us* from *them*, just as Monty Python's Knights of Ni cemented their brotherhood by affirming that they are the knights who say 'ni'.

If all this is right, then the death of God is far from being a threat to ethics. It is a necessary clearing of the ground, on the way to revealing ethics for what it really is. Perhaps there cannot be laws without a lawgiver. But Plato tells us that the ethical laws cannot be the arbitrary whims of personalized Gods. Perhaps instead we can make our own laws. We know that this is sometimes true—there is no biblical or Koranic authority for a 30 mph speed limit—so why shouldn't it always be true?

2. The threat of relativism

So instead of anything with supernatural authority, perhaps we are faced simply with rules of our own making. Then the thought arises that the rules may be made in different ways by different people at different times. In which case, it seems to follow that there is no one truth in ethics. There are only the different truths of different communities. This is the idea of relativism.

Relativism gets a very bad press from most moral philosophers. Yet there is a very attractive side to relativism, which is its association with toleration of different ways of living. Nobody is comfortable now with the blanket colonial certainty that just our way of doing things is right, and that other people need forcing into those ways. It is good that the 19th-century alliance between the missionary and the police has more or less vanished. A more pluralistic and relaxed appreciation of human diversity is often a welcome antidote to an embarrassing imperialism.

The classic statement occurs in Book III of Herodotus's *Histories*. The Greek historian (from the 5th century BC) is criticizing King Cambyses, son of Cyrus of Persia, who showed insufficient respect to Persian laws:

> Everything goes to make me certain that Cambyses was completely mad; otherwise he would not have gone in for mocking religion and tradition. If one were to order all mankind to choose the best set of rules in the world, each group would, after due consideration, choose its own customs; each group regards its own as being by far the best. So it is unlikely that anyone except a madman would laugh at such things.
>
> There is plenty of other evidence to support the idea that this opinion of one's own customs is universal, but here is one instance. During Darius's reign, he invited some Greeks who were present to a conference, and asked them how much money it would take for them to be prepared to eat the corpses of their fathers; they replied that they would not do that for any amount of money. Next, Darius summoned some members of the Indian tribe known as Callatiae, who eat their parents, and asked them in the presence of the Greeks, with an interpreter present so that they could understand what was being said, how much money it would take for them to be willing to cremate their fathers' corpses; they cried out in horror and told him not to say such appalling things. So these practices have become enshrined as customs just as they are, and I think Pindar was right to have said in his poem that custom is king of all.

There are two rather different elements here. One is that the law of custom is all that there is. The other is that the law of custom deserves such respect that only those who are raving mad will mock it. In our moral climate, many people find it easier to accept the first than the second. They suppose that if our standards of conduct are 'just ours' then that strips them of any real authority. We might just as well do things differently, and if we come to do so there is neither real gain nor real loss. What is just or right in the eyes of one people may not be so in the eyes of another, and neither side can claim real truth, unique truth, for its particular rules. Arguing about ethics is arguing about the place at the end of the rainbow: something which is one thing from one point of view, and another from another. A different way of putting it would be that any particular set of standards is purely conventional, where the idea of convention implies that there are other equally proper ways of doing things, but that we just happen to have settled on one of them. As the philosopher says in Tom Stoppard's play *Jumpers*, 'Certainly a tribe which believes it confers honour on its elders by eating them is going to be viewed askance by another which prefers to buy them a little bungalow somewhere.'

Why then does Herodotus show such scorn of Cambyses? Perhaps he was thinking like this. It is conventional to drive on either the right or the left, since each is an equally good solution to the problem of coordinating which side we drive. But it is necessary for there to be *some* rule, and hence there is nothing at all to mock about whichever one we have hit upon. So just *because* of that, a latter-day Cambyses who mocked our slavish obedience to the one rule or the other would be mad.

Now however there come into view norms or standards that are transcultural. In the United States and Europe they drive on the right and in Britain and Australia on the left, but in each country there has to be one rule, or chaos reigns and traffic grinds to a halt. Funerary practices certainly vary, as Darius showed, but perhaps in every community, ever since we stopped dragging our knuckles, there have been needs and emotions that require satisfying by *some* ritual of passing. In Sophocles' tragedy *Antigone* the heroine is torn between two unyielding demands: she must obey the king, who has forbidden burial to his dead opponents in battle, and she must properly bury her brother who was among them. The second demand wins, and not only the ancient Greeks, but we today, understand why. The play translates. Antigone's sense of what needs doing strikes a chord with everyone.

If everybody needs the rule that there should be some rule, that itself represents a universal standard. It can then be suggested that the core of ethics is universal in just this way. Every society that is recognizably human will need some institution of property (some distinction between 'mine' and 'yours'), some standards governing truth-telling, some conception of promise-giving, some restraints on violence and killing. It will need some devices for regulating sexual expression, some sense of what is appropriate by way of treating strangers, or women, or children, or the aged, or the handicapped. It will need some sense of how to distribute resources, and how to treat those who have none. In other words, across the whole spectrum of life, it will need some sense of what is expected and what is out of line. For human beings, there is no living without standards of living.

We can approach the idea of universality a different way, however. We said above that toleration is often a good, and we do well to put many imperialistic certainties behind us. When in Rome do as the Romans do—but what if the Romans go in for some rather nasty doings (as in fact they did)? We do not have to lift the lid very far to find societies whose norms allow the systematic mistreatment of many groups. There are slave-owning societies and caste societies, societies that tolerate widow-burning, or enforce female genital mutilation, or systematically deny education and other rights to women. There are societies where there is no freedom of political expression, or whose treatment of criminals cannot be thought of without a shudder, or where distinctions of religion or language bring with them distinctions of legal and civil status.

Here we have a clash. On the one hand there is the relativist thought that 'If they do it that way, it's OK for them and in any event none of my business.' On the other there is the strong feeling most of us have that these things just should not happen, and we should not stand idly by while they do. We have only perverted or failed solutions to the problems of which standards to implement, if the standards end up like that.

Here it is natural to look to the language of justice and of 'rights'. There are human rights, which these practices flout and deny. But the denial of rights is everybody's concern. If young children are denied education but exploited for labour, or if, as in North African countries, young girls are terrifyingly and painfully mutilated so that thereafter they cannot enjoy natural and pleasurable human sexuality, that is not OK, anywhere or any time. If *they* do it, then *we* have to be against *them*, in attitude and disapproval, even if not in practical political ways.

Many people will want to take such a stand, but then they get confused and defeated by the relativistic thought that, even as we say this, it is still 'just us'. The moral expressions of the last two paragraphs embody good, liberal, Western standards. They are cemented in documents such as the United Nations Declaration of Human Rights. But are they any more than just ours, just now? And if we cannot see them as more than that, then who are we to impose them on others? Multiculturalism seems to block well-meaning liberalism.

We can, of course, insist on our standards, or thump the table. But we want to think of ourselves as doing no *more* than thumping the table, or there will be a little voice saying that we are 'merely' imposing our views or our wills on the others. Table-thumping displays our confidence, but it will not silence the relativistic imp on our shoulders. This is illustrated by a nice anecdote of a friend of mine. He was present at a high-powered ethics institute which had put on a forum in which representatives of the great religions held a panel. First the Buddhist talked of the ways to calm, the mastery of desire, the path of enlightenment, and the panellists all said, 'Wow, terrific, if that works for you that's great.' Then the Hindu talked of the cycles of suffering and birth and rebirth, the teachings of Krishna and the way to release, and they all said, 'Wow, terrific, if that works for you that's great.' And so on, until the Catholic priest talked of the message of Jesus Christ, the promise of salvation, and the way to life eternal, and they all said, 'Wow, terrific, if that works for you that's great.' And he thumped the table and shouted: 'No! It's not a question of if it works for me! It's the true word of the living God, and if you don't believe it you're all damned to Hell!'

And they all said: 'Wow, terrific, if that works for you that's great.'

The joke here lies in the mismatch between what the priest intends—a claim to unique authority and truth—and what he is heard as offering, which is a particular avowal, satisfying to himself, but only to be tolerated or patronized, like any other. The moral is that once a relativist frame of mind is really in place no claims to truth, authority, certainty, or necessity will be audible except as one more saying like all the others. Of course that person talks of certainty and truth, says the relativist. That's just his certainty and truth, made absolute for him, which means no more than: made into his fetish.

Can we find arguments to unseat the relativist's frame of mind? Can we do more than thump the table? If we cannot, does that mean we have to stop thumping it? We return to these questions in section 3 of this book. Meanwhile, here are two thoughts to leave with. The first counteracts the idea that we are just 'imposing' parochial, Western standards when, in the name of universal human rights, we oppose oppressions of people on grounds of gender, caste, race, or religion. Partly, we can say that it is usually not a question of imposing anything. It is a question of cooperating with the oppressed and supporting their emancipation. And it is usually not at all certain that the values we are upholding are so very alien to the others (this is one of the places where we are let down by thinking simplistically of hermetically sealed cultures: *them* and *us*). After all, it is typically only the oppressors who are spokespersons for *their* culture or *their* ways of doing it. It is not the slaves who value slavery, or the women who value the fact that they may not take employment, or the young girls who value disfigurement. It is the brahmins, mullahs, priests, and elders who hold themselves to be spokesmen for *their* culture. What the rest think about it all too often goes unrecorded. Just as victors write the history, so it is those on top who write their justification for the top being where it is. Those on the bottom don't get to say anything.

The second thought is this. Relativism taken to its limit becomes subjectivism: not the view that each culture or society has its own truth, but that each individual has his or her own truth. And who is to say which is right? So, when at the beginning of section 1 I offered some moral remarks about the Old and New Testaments I can imagine someone shrugging: 'Well, that's just your opinion.' It is curious how popular this response is in moral discussions. For notice that it is a conversation-stopper rather than a move in the intended conversation. It is not a reason for or against the proffered opinion, nor is it an invitation for the speaker's reasons, nor any kind of persuasion that it is better to think something else. Anyone sincere is of course voicing their own opinion—that's a tautology (what else could they be doing?). But the opinion is put forward into the public arena. It is something to be agreed with, or at any rate to be taken seriously or weighed for what it is by the audience. The speaker is saying: 'This is my opinion, and here are the reasons for it, and if you have reasons against it we had better look at them...' If the opinion is to be rejected, the next move should be 'No, you shouldn't think that because...'

Sometimes, indeed, ethical conversations need stopping. We are getting nowhere, we agree to differ. But not always. Sometimes we shouldn't stop, and sometimes we cannot risk stopping. If my wife thinks guests ought to be allowed to smoke, and I think they ought not, we had better talk it through and do what we can to persuade the other or find a compromise. The alternatives may be force or divorce, which are a lot worse. And in our practice, if not in our reflections, we all know this. The freshman relativists who say, 'Well it's just your opinion' one moment, will demonstrate the most intense attachment to a particular opinion the next, when the issue is veganism, or preventing vivisection, or shaming sex pests—something they care about.

It is my opinion, but it isn't just my opinion that there needs to be a rule about which side of the road to drive upon. The question would be, what is wrong with someone who cannot see that?

3. The threat of egoism

We are pretty selfish animals. Perhaps it is worse than that: perhaps we are totally selfish animals. Perhaps concern for others, or concern for principle, is a sham. Perhaps ethics needs unmasking. It is just the whistle on the engine, not the steam that actually moves it.

How can we tell? Let us think about method for a moment. On the face of it, there are two fairly good methods for finding what people actually care about. The first is to ask them, and gauge the sincerity of their response and the plausibility of what they say. But people may deceive us, hoping to appear different from what they are. And they may be deceived about themselves. Self-knowledge is an achievement, and perhaps a rare one, as the injunction on the famous oracle at Delphi, 'Know thyself', suggests.

The second method is to look at what they choose and prefer. This too is fallible for people may disguise their preferences. But in general we can check on what people are like by seeing what they do. A man may present himself as a dutiful and nurturing father, and believe himself to be such. But if he never makes or takes an opportunity to be with his children, we have our doubts. Suppose, though, he does make such opportunities, and gladly takes them, and shows few or no regrets for what other pleasures he may be missing by taking them? Then the thing is settled: he cares about his children. In other cases, the diagnosis of smoke screen and hypocrisy beckons. Many governments use the rhetoric of moral duty, civilized missions, and the rest in order to sound good about putting peace-keepers into many of the countries to whom they regularly and copiously sell arms. It is not too difficult to see the mask of concern for what it is.

Does our nurturing father really care for his children? Fallibility still threatens. Life and literature throw up cases where everything looks in line with one interpretation, yet the truth is different. Maybe this model father is scared of his wife, and knows that behaviour that apparently indicates concern for his children is what she expects. Or he may be scared of public opinion, or be angling for a certain kind of reputation to further his commercial or political career. We can look at the settled pattern of his behaviour as well as his sayings, and still wonder whether things are as they seem.

We can, but again we have methods to follow. Suppose the man's wife disappears, or his political career dies but he goes on nurturing as before. This rules out the idea that it was fear of his wife or hope of office that motivated him. The natural interpretation, that he cares for the children and enjoys being with them, is the only one to survive.

In the 19th and 20th centuries scepticism about these homely methods began to loom large, propelled particularly by Marx,

Nietzsche, and Freud. People bowed before the idea of hidden and unconscious meanings, uncovered only by a large-scale theory of human nature. To the theorist's eye things may be a long way from what they seem. So we get the view that pacifism conceals aggression, or a desire to help masks a desire for power, or politeness is an expression of contempt, or contented celibacy expresses a raging desire to procreate. Perhaps everything comes down to sex, or status, or power, or death—a theorist's suspicion is often very good at one-word diagnoses. It is also good at one-word dismissals of any rejection of its one-word solutions: the truth is repressed; it is hidden by false consciousness. In fact, the subject's resistance to any proffered reinterpretation can become an index of how true it is. The ideology becomes closed.

A surprising theory can go along with good insights. It can unify otherwise disparate and puzzling human phenomena. In his famous book *The Theory of the Leisure Class* (1899), the sociologist Thorstein Veblen noticed a whole slew of strange facts along the following lines. First, itinerant workers who earn reasonable money tend to be 'showy', carrying flashy jewellery and large bankrolls, going in for high-stake poker games, and the like. Rooted peasants who could easily afford it never do so. Second, people deplore the taste of others who are just a little beneath them in wealth and social status, more than they deplore the taste of those a long way beneath them. Third, an aristocrat will prefer an able-bodied man as a butler or footman, rather than a female or someone handicapped who could do the job equally well. Fourth, a well-kept lawn or park is a good thing round a nice house.

Veblen unified these odd facts and many others with the theory that people have a need for wasteful display in order to manifest their status. Unlike the rooted countryman the itinerant has to display this status on his person, and hence the flashy appearance. We need to shout that we are not like those just beneath us on the social ladder, for whom we might be mistaken, more than we need to shout that we are not like those a long way beneath us, for whom we won't be mistaken. The aristocrat can better signal plenty by keeping able-bodied servants in unproductive jobs than if he keeps otherwise unemployable ones in such positions. Hence footmen and butlers. Similarly with gardens, lawns, and parks, which are beautiful just because they are ornamental and unproductive (Veblen thought the need controls aesthetic judgements as well). Veblen's insight is often summed up as the doctrine of 'conspicuous consumption'. But the label is in fact a misnomer. The rooted peasant does not consume conspicuously. He does not have to, just because everyone he cares about knows to within an atom what he is worth.

The view that consumption has a lot more to do with vanity or status than we might have supposed is immediately plausible and was anticipated by many other thinkers, including Adam Smith (1723–90) (in spite of his rightly revered stature as a pioneering economist, Smith, who was first a moral philosopher, took a very dim view of the desire for wealth and status). And once Veblen has stated it in a more precise form, we can test it against our own experience and find if it works. It has the hallmarks of a good scientific theory. It is simple. It gives a unified explanation of otherwise diverse and disconnected patterns of behaviour. It is predictive (for instance, it would predict a pressure on the rooted peasant to put on a suit for his journey to town, where his worth is unknown). As a result it is falsifiable: for we might come across instances where the theory seems not to work, and it would need adjusting or abandoning in the light of them.

Many such theories are not so well favoured. Let us return to the dispiriting view that everybody always acts out of their own self-interest. It can be very unclear what this means, but taken at face value it is obviously false. People *neglect* their own interest or *sacrifice* their own interest to other passions and concerns. This neglect or sacrifice need not even be high-minded: the moralist Joseph Butler (1692–1752) gives the example of a man who runs

23

upon certain ruin in order to avenge himself for an insult. Friends with his interests at heart might try to dissuade him, but fail. What this man may need to do is to act *more* out of self-interest, so that anticipating his ruin checks his desire for revenge. But if his desire had been for the welfare of others, or for the preservation of the rain forest, or for the reduction of third-world debt, the fact that he was neglecting or sacrificing his own interests might have seemed irrelevant. It is what the situation calls for in his eyes, and if we share his standards, perhaps in ours as well. If he spends his fortune or ruins his health on these objects, he may regard himself as only having done what he had to do.

There is a trick to be guarded against at this point. Someone might read the last paragraph and complain: 'That is all very well if we think of someone's self-interest only in terms of money, or career, or even health. Certainly, people sacrifice these to other concerns. But then we just have agents whose *real* interests or full self-interest include these other things: the revenge or the rain forest or the third-world debt. They are still just as self-interested as anyone else.' The reason this is a trick is that it empties the view of all content. It kidnaps the word 'self-interest' for *whatever* the agent is concerned about. But just for that reason it loses any predictive or explanatory force. With this understanding of interest or self-interest you could never say, 'Watch, the agent won't do this but will do that because, like all agents, she acts out of self-interest.' All you can do is wait to see what the agent in fact does, and then read back and boringly announce that this is where her interests lay. The move is not only boring but a nuisance, since, as Butler puts it, this is not the language of mankind. It would have us saying that if I stand back in order for the women and children to get in the lifeboat, then my self-interest lay in their being in the lifeboat rather than me. And this is just not the way we describe such an action. It appears to add a cynical reinterpretation of the agent, but in fact adds nothing but confusion.

Perhaps surprisingly, we can see the general falsity of egoism by thinking of particular cases where it is indeed true. These are cases where an appearance of some larger concern does in fact disguise self-interest. Suppose two people give to a charity. Suppose it comes out that the charity is corrupt, and proceeds do not go to the starving poor but to the directors. And suppose that on receiving this news the first person is irritated and angry, not so much at the directors of the charity, but at the person bringing the news ('Why bring this up? Just let me be'). Whereas the second person is indignant at the directors themselves. Then we can reasonably suggest that the first person prized his own peace of mind or reputation for generosity, more than he cared about the starving poor. Whereas the second has a more genuine concern for what goes on in the world, not for whether he is comfortable or how he stands in the eyes of others.

Fortunately, however, we are not all like the first person, or not all the time. We can be indignant at the directors, just as we are indignant at many things that go on around us. We don't always shoot the messenger, and we can want to be told the truth because it is a truth that concerns us. We return to the emergence of cooperation later, in section 12.

4. The threat from evolutionary theory

There has existed a vague belief that some combination of evolutionary theory, biology, and neuroscience will support a general egoism. Indeed, most of the popular books on ethics in the bookstores fall into one of two camps. There are those that provide chicken soup for the soul: soggy confections of consolation and uplift. Or, there are those that are written by one or another life-scientist: a neuroscientist or biologist or animal behaviourist or evolutionary theorist anxious to tell that 'science' has shown that we are all one thing or another. Once more we stand unmasked: human beings are 'programmed'. Often we are egoists, altruism doesn't exist, ethics is only a fig-leaf for selfish strategies; we are all conditioned, women are nurturing, men are rapists, we care above all for our genes.

There is good news and bad news about the popularity of this genre. The good news is that we do have a relentless appetite for self-interpretation. There is a huge desire to find patterns of behaviour, enabling us to understand ourselves and others better, and even perhaps to control the human flux. The bad news is the extent to which we will accord authority to anyone in a white coat, even when the science is over (for as we are about to see, talking of the significance of science is not talking science).

We should only venture into this literature if we are armed against three confusions. The first is this. It is one thing to explain how we come to be as we are. It is a different thing to say that we are different from what we think we are. Yet these are fatally easy to confuse together. Suppose, for instance, evolutionary theory tells us that mother-love is an adaptation. This means that it has been 'selected for', because animals in which it exists reproduce and spread their genetic material more successfully than ones in which it does not. We could, if we like, imagine a 'gene for mother-love'. Then the claim would be that animals with this gene are and have been more successful than animals having only a variant (an allele) that does not code for mother-love. The confusion would be to infer that *therefore* there is not really any such thing as mother-love: thus we unmask it! The confusion is to infer that underneath the mask we are only concerned to spread genetic material more successfully.

Not only does this not follow, but it actually contradicts the starting point. The starting point is 'Mother-love exists, and this is why'; the conclusion is that mother-love doesn't exist.

In other words an evolutionary story, plausible or not, about the genetic function of a trait such as mother-love must not be confused with a psychological story unmasking a mother's 'real

26

concern'. Perhaps nobody would make this mistake so baldly in this instance. But consider the idea of 'reciprocal altruism'. Game theorists and biologists noticed that animals frequently help each other when it would seem to be to their advantage not to do so. They asked the perfectly good question of how such behaviour could have evolved, when it looks set to lose out to a more selfish strategy. The answer is (or may be) that it is adaptive insofar as it triggers reciprocal helping behaviour from the animal helped, or from others witnessing the original event. In other words, we have a version of 'You scratch my back and I'll scratch yours'.

The explanation may be perfectly correct. It may provide the reason why we ourselves have inherited altruistic tendencies. The confusion strikes again, however, when it is inferred that altruism doesn't *really* exist, or that we don't *really* care disinterestedly for one another—we only care to maximize our chance of getting a return on our investments of helping behaviour. The mistake is just the same—inferring that the psychology is not what it seems because of its functional explanation—but it seems more seductive here, probably because we fear that the conclusion is true more often in this case than in the case of motherhood. There are indeed cases of seeming altruism disguising hope for future benefits. But there are of course cases in which it is not like this, and shown to be such by the methods of the last section. The driver gives the penniless hitch-hiker a lift; the diner tips the waiter he knows he will never see again; they each do it when there are no bystanders to watch the action.

To guard against this confusion, contemplate sexual desire. It has an adaptive function, presumably, which is the propagation of the species. But it is completely off-the-wall to suppose that those in the grip of sexual desire 'really' want to propagate the species. Most of the time many of us emphatically do not—otherwise there would be no birth control, elderly sex, homosexuality, solitary sex, and other variations—and many people never do. Some moralists might wish it were otherwise, but it isn't.

So, this first confusion is to infer that our apparent concerns are not our real concerns, simply from the fact of an evolutionary explanation of them.

The second confusion is to infer the impossibility that such-and-such a concern should exist, from the fact that we have no evolutionary explanation for it. This is unwarranted, for it may well be that there is no evolutionary explanation for all kinds of quirks: no explanation for why we enjoy birdsong, or like the taste of cinnamon, or have ticklish feet. These traits may just be side-effects of others that are adaptive, or they may be descendants of traits that were once adaptive but are so no longer, or they may be nothing to do with adaptations, but just due to chance. Or they may be adaptations but only because they affect the 'eye of the beholder': perhaps it is more pleasurable to be with a partner who has ticklish feet, and then a mechanism of 'sexual selection' kicks in to boost the prevalence of the trait. That throws us back onto the question of why the pleasure and the preference exists, but perhaps it just does. Female peacocks go for the huge, beautiful, but apparently dysfunctional tails of the male, and female Irish elks went for the male practically immobilized by the biggest antlers. It is not easy to see why, and this problem can unfit explanations in terms of sexual selection, for some purposes. For instance, if we find the human propensity for art or music puzzling, because we cannot find a survival function for it, it doesn't immediately help to suggest that females prefer artistic and musical men, since we won't be able to find a survival function for that female preference, either. What this means is that the explanation has to continue. It might continue by showing that females recognize that artistry and musicianship indicate *other* survival-enhancing traits, such as industry or cunning, and perhaps the peacock's gaudy tail may indicate freedom from disease, or the elk's antlers indicate its strength. Or, it might postulate a 'trembling hand'—a random jerk in the evolutionary process, such as the inaccurate copying of a gene, that just happened to entrench itself.

The third confusion to guard against is to read psychology into nature, and in particular into the gene, and then read it back into the person whose gene it is. The most notorious example of this mistake is due to *The Selfish Gene* by Richard Dawkins. Here the fact that genes, like viruses, replicate and have a different chance of replicating in different environments is presented metaphorically in terms of their being 'selfish' and indulging a kind of ruthless competition to beat out other genes. It is then fatally easy to infer that the human animal must itself be selfish, since somehow this is the only appropriate psychology for the vehicle in which these little monsters are carried. Or at least, if we are not selfish, it is because by some strange miracle we can transcend and fight off the genetic pressure to be so. Dawkins first advanced, but has since repudiated, this idea, yet it maintains a life of its own.

Genes are not selfish any more than viruses are—they just have different chances of replicating themselves in different environments. Not only may they do better if the person carrying them is unselfish, altruistic, and principled, but it is easy to see why this should be so. As Darwin himself saw, a society of unselfish, altruistic, and principled persons is obviously set to do better than a group in which there are none of these traits, but only a 'war of all against all'. Furthermore, the environment in which we human beings flourish is largely a social environment. We succeed in the eyes of each other. Hence, a principle like that of sexual selection kicks in: if these are traits we admire in each other, they are likely to be successful not only for the society as a whole, but also for any individual who has them. And we do admire them.

Biological thinking has itself evolved beyond the ideological image of relentless competition in the jungle for survival. The present century has witnessed a decline of that ideology, and a substitute in terms of coordination and cooperation. At every level in the biosphere, from the interaction of cells up to and including the interactions of humans, symbiosis—the need to work and live together—is far more significant in the race of life than competition. Again, we return to this in section 12.

5. The threat of determinism and futility

Another implication of the life sciences that threatens ethics, in many people's minds, is the threat of determinism. The idea here is that since it is 'all in the genes' the enterprise of ethics becomes hopeless. The basket of motivations that in fact move people may not be simple, but its contents in any particular person may be fixed. And then we just do as we are programmed to do. It is no use railing about it or regretting it: we cannot kick against nature.

This raises the whole thorny topic of free will. Here, I want to look at only one particular version of the problem. This takes our genetic make-up to imply the futility of ethics, meaning in particular the futility of moral advice or education or experience. The threat is the paralysing effect of realizing that we are what we are: large mammals, made in accordance with genetic instructions about which we can do nothing.

A moral enterprise might indeed be hopeless because it tries to alter fixed nature. A prohibition on long hair may be enforceable, say in the army or the police force. But a prohibition on growing hair at all is not, since we are indeed programmed to do it. An order forbidding hunger or thirst (or, in the army, an order against dying of heat or cold) is futile, since we cannot control such things. Some cases are less clear. Imagine a particularly ascetic monastic order, whose rule not only enjoins chastity, but forbids sexual desire. On the face of it the rule is futile. It cannot be obeyed because it is not up to us whether we feel sexual desire. At the right time the hormones boil, and sexual desire bubbles up (lust was an object of particular horror to early Christian moralists just because of its 'rebellious' or involuntary nature). The chemical instructions are genetically encoded. There may indeed be marginal technologies of control: yoga, or biofeedback, or drugs. But for most young people most of the time, any injunction not to feel desire is laughable. But this is not to say that the embargo has no effect at all. It may well do so. It may bring shame and embarrassment to those who find that they cannot conform to it. This may even be its concealed function, since it may thereby reinforce their subservience in the face of the implacable authority that commanded it. It can increase the power of churches or parents to keep their dependants in a state of guilt or a state of shame. But the rule is directly futile: it cannot be obeyed. So the question is, are all rules similarly futile, because of genetic determinism?

The answer is no, because whatever our genetic make-up programmes us to do, it leaves room for us to vary our behaviour in response to what we hear or feel or touch or see (otherwise there would be little point in having these senses in the first place). It leaves room for us to vary our desires in accordance with what we learn (discovering that the glass contains sulphuric acid, I lose the desire to drink it that I had when I thought it contained gin). It leaves room for us to be influenced by information gathered from others.

If we liked paradox, we might put this baldly by saying that genetics programmes us to be flexible. But there is no paradox really. Even an inanimate structure that is literally programmed can be made to be flexible. A chess programme will be designed to give a different response depending on what move its opponent has just made. It is input-responsive. Inflexible traits (growing hair, getting thirsty) are not input-responsive because no matter what beliefs, desires, or attitudes we have, they go on just the same. But many of our own beliefs and desires and attitudes are not like that. They show endless plasticity. They vary with our surroundings, including the moral climate in which we find ourselves.

It is an empirical matter how flexible we are in any particular respect. So genetic theory cannot forbid us from recognizing that a child may be disposed to become kind and loving in a kind and loving environment, vicious and aggressive in a vicious and aggressive one, intellectual or musical in an intellectual or musical one. And these dispositions may in turn be liable to be displaced if other factors influence things. We just have to look and see.

Very possibly, what we may find is greater receptivity at some stages, and relative inflexibility thereafter. If this is so, far from sidelining the importance of the moral environment, the excursus through determinism will catapult it to the head of the agenda. That is where it should be if, once we have been weaned into an atmosphere of violence, aggression, insensitivity, sentimentality, manipulation, and furtiveness—the everyday world of politics and entertainments, for example—we can never or almost never climb out.

There are other threats of futility than genetic determinism. There is the mood in which all human life is futile. I discuss this in more detail later.

6. The threat of unreasonable demands

I have argued for moderate optimism about human nature, at least blocking the pessimisms and reinterpretations that we have met so far. But we have to be realistic, and we should not demand too much from ourselves and each other.

Then the threat arises that ethics does just that, and not in some overblown, over-demanding version, but at its very core. And then we get the reaction that 'it's all very well in principle, but in practice it just won't work'. As Kant remarked, this is 'said in a lofty, disdainful tone, full of the presumption of wanting to reform reason by experience'. Kant finds it especially offensive, contrasting the 'dim, moles' eyes fixed on experience' with 'the eyes belonging to a being that was made to stand erect and look at the heavens'.

However the threat is real, and we can consider several versions of it. First, consider a morality centred on a simple and abstract set of rules. One of them may be 'Thou shalt not lie.' Now of course when we think of central examples of this rule, we are apt to approve of it. We should not abuse other people's trust in us, and a deliberate, manipulative, bare-faced lie may well do that. But there are other cases. There are white lies, socially expected and condoned. There are lies told to people who shouldn't be asking, because it is none of their business and they have no right to the truth, or even because telling them the truth would bring catastrophe. It was one of the less palatable consequences of Kant's own rule-bound system that he didn't admit these as valid excuses. He thought it was impermissible to lie to the mad axeman who asks you where your children are sleeping although such a person would have no right to the truth and it would be catastrophic to inform him. There are also lies told in the service of a greater truth. 'There is no danger' may be literally false, but said by the pilot it puts the passengers in a more appropriate frame of mind than 'The risk is quite small.' There are lies we perhaps in desperation tell ourselves, and get to believe, before we tell others ('It's not the harmful kind of cancer, dear').

It was central to Kant's moral scheme that the prohibition against lying remained simple and absolute: no exceptions. Suppose we agree with him. Then a perfectly reasonable reaction from anyone muddling along in society, or from the mother facing the axe-man, or from the pilot calming the passengers, would be 'To hell with that. If *that's* what morality demands, then I'm opting out.'

Here is a second example where the stringency of ethics can lead to its rejection. Many theories of ethics highlight the *impartial* and *universal* nature of the moral point of view. It is a point of view that treats everyone equally: every person has equal weight.

Unless there are further factors, it is no better, from the moral point of view, that I should have some goods and you should not than that you should have them, and I should not. If the person without the goods is starving, and the person with them has plenty, then morality demands a split: the money is needed more by the starving. The starvation of the poor requires redistribution from the rich. For many people, our duty to leave a decent physical environment for our successors requires giving up travel, heating, the use of plastic, or the eating of meat.

Few manage the lifestyle that conforms to these real ideals for it is easy to preach such things, but much harder to practise them. Indeed the most blatant hypocrisies of our times include the comfortable academic arguing that justice is not served unless we have voluntary or involuntary redistribution programmes which carve the entire cake equally, the pampered first-world student littering Glastonbury with discarded plastic while preaching ecological absolutism, and the celebrities and princes flying around in private jets preaching against global warming. Even when at some level we accept that morality demands some of these things of us, a natural reaction is to shrug off its demands. It's not going to happen; it's impractical; we can ignore it.

I do not think it is easy to find a stable attitude to the stringency of the prohibition on lying, or still more to the duty of concern for others, including future generations. But I do think something has gone wrong if *extreme* demands are placed squarely in the centre of ethics. The centre of ethics must be occupied by things we can *reasonably* demand of each other. The absoluteness of the fanatic, or the hair shirt of the saint, lie on the outer shores. Not wanting to follow them there, or even not able to do so, we still have plenty of standards left to uphold. We should still want to respond to the reasonable demands of decency. We may not be able to solve all the world's problems, but we should do our best with the ones we can solve. So the right reaction is to look for moral principles that are not impractical, and not limitless in their demands. Adhering to anything more stringent might be saintly, and admirable, but it is not *demanded* of us. In the standard phrase, it is above and beyond the call of duty.

A different example of a bid to escape the stringency of behaving well is the excuse of 'dirty hands'. It's a bad business manufacturing arms, or selling cattle prods and handcuffs to various regimes. But, says the manufacturer (or the government), if we don't do it someone else will. Then they have the jobs and reap the rewards. The arms and prods and handcuffs get made just the same, so why should we sacrifice our well-being for the benefit of our competitors? The moralist, standing erect and looking at the heavens, is simply out of touch with the need to make a living. Ethics is all very well, but perhaps we cannot afford it. At least with his eyes on the earth the dim mole earns his living.

There is something grubby, not only to Kant but I think to most of us, about the excuse that this argument offers us. We have some sense that we should keep our own hands clean, however much others will then dirty theirs. The excuse is not open to a person of strict honour or integrity, however convenient it may be in practice. In many areas, it is not over and above the call of duty to keep our own hands clean.

7. The threat of false consciousness

In sections 3 and 4 we met theories that tried to discover hidden unconscious motivations, things that really move us, leaving ethical concerns exposed as mere whistles on the engine. We resisted their claims. But there is still room to argue that the social role of morality is tainted. Even if the motivations of its practitioners are sincere enough, this is because such people have been somehow sucked into a system. And the system may not be what it seems.

Consider, for instance, a feminist criticism of a piece of male behaviour. The man holds open a door for the woman, or offers to carry her parcel, or gives up a seat for her. A feminist may find this offensive. She does not have to say that the man intends to demean the woman. His behaviour, the feminist may maintain, is part of a 'system' or 'institution' or 'pattern' of such events whose net effect is a signal that women are weaker or in need of male protection. And this is what she finds offensive. Of course, the man in turn may find her offence offensive, and up start political correctness wars and gender wars.

The feminist may go in for the kind of hidden psychological theories we have met, saying that the man unconsciously intends to demean the woman. But that is unnecessary. She need not work at the level of individual psychology. All she has to say is that the man behaves as he does because of a system or socially institutionalized set of behaviours that are entrenched in the society, and that the upshot of the system is to demean women. This is enough for her critique to gain a hold.

For another example of this kind of critique, imagine a sincere cleric wringing his hands over his parishioners' sins. He is genuinely upset. He believes they are doing wrong, and fears for their souls. His heart goes out to them. There is nothing, so far, wrong with him. But he may be a part of a system with a rather more sinister function for all that. The Church that taught him may be an organization dedicated to its own power, and as we already suggested, controlling people's sense of shame and guilt and sin is an instrument of power. It probably works best if nobody from the Pope down to the individual cleric realizes that, either consciously or unconsciously.

So a critic might now suggest that ethics as an institution (I shall write this, Ethics) is a system whose real function is other than it seems. A feminist might see it as an instrument of patriarchal oppression. A Marxist can see it as an instrument of class oppression. A Nietzschean may see it as a lie with which the feeble and timid console themselves for their inability to seize life as it should be seized. A modern French philosopher, such as Michel Foucault, can see it as a diffuse exercise of power and control. In any event, it stands unmasked.

There may be a good deal of truth in some of these critiques. We can think of local elements of morality, at particular places and times, that certainly seem open to some such diagnosis. The passion with which the rich defend the free market can invite the raised eyebrow. A morality that gives *us* the right to *their* land, or the right to kill *them* for not having the same rituals as *us*, invites a similar diagnosis. The self-serving nature of systems of religion, or caste systems, or patriarchal or market systems, can be almost entirely hidden from view to those who practise them.

There is something a little off colour as well about some of the ways morality sometimes intrudes into people's lives. The judge, the priest, or the elders, a panel of the great and the good, may tell people what they must do—but themselves they do not usually have to live with the consequences. If the girl was not allowed the abortion, or the family not allowed to assist the suicide, they have to pick up the pieces and soldier on themselves, perhaps in prison. Those who told them how they had to behave can go on lunching at the club. An impartial moral law can bear very unevenly on different people, and it is little wonder if people become disenchanted by an ethics largely maintained by those who do not have 'skin in the game', do not have to live it. Similarly, Anatole France spoke of the 'majestic equality of the laws which forbid rich and poor alike to sleep under bridges, to beg in the streets, and to steal bread'.

But although we may well accept examples of this kind of critique, I don't think it could possibly be generalized to embrace all of ethics. The reason is implicit in what we have already said: for human beings, there is no living without standards of living. This means that ethics is not Ethics: it is not an 'institution' or organization with sinister hidden purposes that might be better unmasked. It is not the creature of some concealed conspiracy by 'them': Society, or The System, or The Patriarchy. There are indeed institutions, such as the Church or State, that may seek to control our standards, and their nature and function may need to be queried. But that will mean at most a *different* ethic. It does not and cannot introduce the end of ethics.

Central elements of our standards do indeed have a function, and it may be hidden from practitioners. An ordinary person may just be shocked at a broken promise, and that is the end of it. They do not have to reflect on the function of promise-keeping. But if they do reflect, then the point of the 'institution' of promising may come into view. Its point will be something like this. By giving promises we give each other confidence in what we are going to do, thus enabling joint enterprises to go forward. That is a point we can be proud of; without something serving that point, flexible plans for coordinated action become impossible. Here the description of the hidden function is not an 'unmasking' or a deconstruction. If anything it gives a boost to our respect for the norms surrounding promise-keeping. It shows that it is not just something about which we, the bourgeois, have a fetish. As I like to put it, it is not a debunking explanation, but a bunking one.

Other central elements of morality don't even get this kind of explanation. They are less of a human invention than is the device of giving promises. Gratitude to those who have done us good, sympathy with those in pain or in trouble, and dislike of those who delight in causing pain and trouble, are natural to most of us, and are good things. Almost any ethic will encourage them. Here there is nothing to unmask: these are just features of how most of us are, and how all of us are at our best. They are not the result of a conspiracy, any more than the enjoyment of food or the fear of death are: they just define how we live and how we want to live and want others to live. Nietzsche indeed tried to 'deconstruct' the benevolent emotions, railing against them as weak or slavish or life-denying, but the attempt is unconvincing and unpleasant, a kind of Hemingway machismo that regards decent human sympathy as unmanly.

These have been seven threats to thinking about ethics. But there are other obstacles to living ethical lives, which occupy us in Part 3.

Part 2
Foundations

In Part 1, I tried to deflect some of the problems that beset thinking about ethics. But we still have to worry whether our favourite ethical principles are capable of proof. We might still fear that the voice of conscience is a delusion. We might still flounder when we try to gain some sense of its authority. Are truth and knowledge possible, or does reasoning about what to do eventually hinge on nothing but banging the table—sheer brute will? Or are there yet other alternatives?

8. Two species of reason

In order to think about the place of reason in ethics, we need to make a distinction. A Holy Grail in practical philosophy would be a reason that everyone *must* acknowledge to be a reason, independently of their sympathies and inclinations. I shall call that a Reason, with a capital letter. It would armlock everyone. You could not ignore it or discount it just because you feel differently. It would have a necessary influence, or what philosophers sometimes call 'apodictic' force. It would bind all rational agents, insofar as they are rational. If you offer someone a reason (no capital letter) and they shrug it off, you might say they are insensitive or inhuman, callous or selfish, obsessive or weird, imprudent or sentimental. These are defects of the heart. You may regret them, but if the audience feels differently you may not be able to prove to them that they are defects at all. But if you offer someone a capital-letter Reason and they shrug it off, then something different is wrong. Their very rationality is in jeopardy. There is something wrong with their heads.

Philosophers, of course, are professionally wedded to reasoning, so it is natural to them to hope that we can find Reasons.

Before the 18th century, many moral philosophers thought that we could. They thought that fundamental principles of ethics could be seen to be true by the 'natural light of reason'. They were 'a priori', having the same kind of certainty as logic, arithmetic, or geometry; you could see from your armchair that they had to be true. If you couldn't see it, then your understanding must be at fault, just as if you can't understand that there is no biggest natural number, or no such thing as a round square. For many such principles were innate, inscribed for us by a benevolent deity, so that ignoring them would be a kind of impiety.

By the end of the 17th century, this theory had lost a lot of ground, especially among philosophers more ready to trust empirical sense experience as a source of knowledge, rather than allegedly divine revelations. If we want provability, it began to be felt, we cannot rely on God to have put it there. But even the great empiricist John Locke (1632–1704) subscribed to a rational foundation for the basic principles of morals:

> ...The idea of a supreme Being, infinite in power, goodness, and wisdom, whose workmanship we are, and on whom we depend; and the idea of ourselves, as understanding, rational creatures, being such as are clear in us, would, I suppose, if duly considered and pursued, afford such foundations of our duty and rules of action as might place morality amongst the sciences capable of demonstration: wherein I doubt not but from self-evident propositions, by necessary consequences, as incontestable as those in mathematics, the measures of right and wrong might be made

out, to any one that will apply himself with the same indifferency
and attention to the one as he does to the other of these sciences.

As this shows however, Locke thought this was something that
could in principle be done, rather than something that had
already been done. And he thought it had to be done with an
excursus through theology, which scarcely inspires confidence.

This view was first challenged in the 18th century by the
'sentimentalists' the Earl of Shaftesbury and Frances Hutcheson,
but then with much greater force by David Hume (1711–76), who
took a dim view about the power of reason anywhere, but
especially here. For Hume, reason's proper sphere is confined to
mathematics and logic, while knowledge about the way things are
is due solely to sense experience. Neither affords us any
substantive principles of conduct. Hence there are no Reasons.
Hume drives the message home flamboyantly:

> Reason is and ought only to be the slave of the passions, and can
> never pretend to any other office than to serve and obey them... Tis
> not contrary to reason to prefer the destruction of the whole world
> to the scratching of my finger. 'Tis not contrary to reason for me to
> choose my total ruin, to prevent the least uneasiness of an Indian or
> person wholly unknown to me. 'Tis as little contrary to reason to
> prefer even my own acknowledged lesser good to my greater...

There is evidence that Hume came to regret the rhetoric in such
passages, and he plays it down when he returns to the issue in
later works that he came to prefer, notably his *Enquiry
Concerning the Principles of Morals*. But he continued to think
that human reason has a limited reach. It includes mathematics
and logic, for if we try to disobey their laws, understanding gives
out and thought itself becomes impossible. We are left with no
ideas at all. And we can talk of the reasonable, or scientific,

approach to understanding the world, which often speaks with one voice, leaving no room for dissent. But when it comes to ethics we are in the domain of what Hume called passion or sentiment, general terms covering desires, attitudes, emotions, and preferences: the practical dispositions that direct our wills. And it sounds as though in this domain the heart rules everything.

That might be misleading. Our passions and sentiments need to operate in the world that we learn about. Mistakes about where we are and what is what is a prelude to acting disastrously, both for ourselves and others. As we shall see in Part 3, an inability to reason properly is as great a recipe for human disasters as actual vice and malevolence. Stupidity is at least as dangerous as sin. But what we incline towards and are motivated to pursue, after reason and experience have done their work, is another thing. Even basic, unambitious concerns, such as self-interest or sympathy, are not mandated by reason alone. If we choose to neglect our own interests we may be feckless and imprudent, but we are not contradicting ourselves. The plight of others gives us reasons to act, certainly, but not Reasons. There may indeed be some formal limits on our preferences: there is something 'irrational' about preferring A to B, and also at the same time preferring B to A. But there are no substantive restrictions on our passions imposed by reason alone.

This could be put in terms of a contrast between *description* and *prescription*. Calculation and basic consistency is involved in getting our descriptions of the world right. What we then prescribe is beyond their jurisdiction. This is what Hume meant by saying that reason is in fact wholly at the service of the passions. The passions, preferences, desires, and attitudes that we have are supremely important, for it is only in order to direct them towards effective action that we need to know anything about the world in the first place.

9. The party of mankind

Suppose we imagine an ordinary, everyday, lower-case reason for having acted a certain way. The everyday reason might be 'I wanted it', or 'I liked him (so I did something for him)', or 'That's what would save the most money'. A reason might be narrowly selfish, or it might be public-spirited: 'It helps to promote the general welfare' or 'It delivers people from horrendous pains and miseries.'

Such reasons can be appealing. If our sympathies lie in the same direction we will appreciate them and accept them, and conversely if they are alien to us we reject them and see those who are swayed by them as unreasonable and perhaps foolish, impetuous, or stupid. They work in many conversations. But there is no proof that they *have* to work. It seems to depend how much the audience sympathizes with us, or with humanity, or feels the same way as us. It seems to depend on our tastes or feelings about things. In his great work *The Theory of Moral Sentiments* Adam Smith happily bit this bullet: his third chapter is entitled 'Of the manner in which we judge of the propriety or impropriety of the Affections of other Men, by their concord or dissonance with our own'. His general mantra is that 'To approve of another man's opinions is to adopt those opinions, and to adopt them is to approve of them.' He recognizes that this is not the whole story, since, for example, if we find a stranger grief-stricken on the death of a loved one we may approve of their grief without ourselves grieving. We cannot feel as the affected party feels, but for all that we sympathize with the grief, supposing that it is what we ourselves would feel in such a place. And it is that conformity that determines our sense that the grief is appropriate; that this person's heart is in the right place. It is this identity of actual and potential sentiments that makes up agreement in our sentiments. And for Smith, like Hume, agreement in ethical and moral matters is entirely a matter of this consilience or identity of sentiment, and argument about ethical matters is a matter of forging such identity.

Of course, not every divergence in how we feel about things has an ethical dimension. There are matters of mere taste or mere preference. You have your tastes, I have mine, and often enough we do not care about the difference. Ethics only rears its head when we feel the need for a common point of view, on matters where anyone else's different sentiments disturb or offend us or stand in the way of what we regard as the thing to do, the way to go.

A natural worry is that Smith is making each person his or her own judge of good and bad, right or wrong. In practice this may be quite realistic about the way moral discussions are conducted, but it seems to leave something missing. Can't we worry whether our own feelings are themselves distorted, or less than admirable in various ways? To avoid this kind of worry Adam Smith softens the egocentric cast of his thought by admitting this self-critical element of human nature. We each have an internalized image of a potential critic. This is the 'man within the breast', the impartial spectator whose witness of our own conduct matters, or should matter, to us.

Many contemporary ethical thinkers suspect that to judge something to be good is equivalent to judging that it is what my 'ideal self' would choose. Adam Smith is both socializing and operationalizing the ideal self. That is, rather than some abstract, vague, and hazy idea of perfection he locates the element of idealization socially, in the idea of the gaze of others. And by doing so he puts flesh and blood on the idea, in the concrete form of impartial scrutiny. It gives him a secularized version of the religious idea of us being open to the scrutiny of the all-seeing eye of God.

The poet Robert Burns, himself an avid fan of Smith, echoed the idea when in his poem 'To a Louse' he lamented that we do not have the gift of seeing ourselves as others see us: 'It would from many a blunder free us, and foolish notion.' We have to admit that to an impartial eye our own peculiarities, including the shape our sentiments take, may look less than lovely. Yet we have to soldier on with the endowment we have, for if we actually judged some sentiment better than our own, then by that very judgement we would be at least on the way towards making it our own. If I really admit that turning right is a better way to go than turning left as I originally intended, then, other things being equal, I turn right.

To these thinkers it wasn't all that difficult to achieve a decent consensus about many issues of ethical importance. They felt able to rely upon a large budget of widely shared sentiments, bedrock elements of almost any unperverted human nature. Hume waxes eloquent on the issue:

> Besides discretion, *caution, enterprise, industry, assiduity, frugality, œconomy, good-sense, prudence, discernment*; besides these endowments, I say, whose very names force an avowal of their merit, there are many others, to which the most determined scepticism cannot, for a moment refuse the tribute of praise and approbation. *Temperance, sobriety, patience, constancy, perseverance, forethought, considerateness, secrecy, order, insinuation, address, presence of mind, quickness of conception, facility of expression*; these, and a thousand more of the same kind, no man will ever deny to be excellencies and perfections.

Equally it would be easy to write a list of things which we would want a decent political ethics to sustain: life, liberty, the pursuit of happiness, freedom from want and insecurity, a polity that gives as many people as possible a basis for self-respect.

Or, we could put it the other way round, by listing vices and flaws to which people are prone, and the ills of life from which we would want a decent political ethics to help to protect us.

For Hume and Smith such shared goals give a sufficient foundation for ethics. They give us an assurance that while we may not be able to 'prove' a moral opinion to any arbitrary sceptic or abandoned villain, we can expect to find opinions that stand up to the scrutiny of what Hume called the 'party of mankind'—the decent people who have internalized a sense of the authority of the impartial spectator, and therefore whose sentiments are sufficiently like our own for conversation to be worth having.

10. Doing good and living well

Reason does not give up its title to sovereignty over practical affairs without a fight. In this section and section 11 I consider two very different kinds of opposition. The first already existed in the Aristotelian thought that the *telos* or goal of a human being is to live a certain kind of life. What kind of life? Obviously one in which certain basic biological needs for food, warmth, shelter, and perhaps sex are met. Aristotle, however, thought that the 'intended' life for a human being was political, in a society or *polis*. And there flourishing requires social virtues. It also connects, he thought, with life lived according to reason. And this may seem to give us a kind of foundation for ethics. The vicious or depraved or insensitive or callous are failing to exercise reason, the supreme human capacity.

But first of all, why think that the 'intended' or natural life for human beings is a life of virtue? On the face of it this equation requires a pretty sunny view of the human animal. It is just a matter of observation that evolution has thrown up a human nature with significant elements of selfishness, aggression, vengefulness, short-sightedness, cruelty, and so forth. And some fairly unpleasant people are healthy, to judge by what Bernard Williams nicely describes as 'the ecological standard of the bright eye and the glossy coat'. Conversely, there may be circumstances, one would think, in which virtue requires us to sacrifice something of our own health or happiness. In the limit, virtue and duty may require us to lay down life itself. So there is no automatic alignment between behaving well and looking after ourselves.

Aristotle himself was not quite as optimistic as it might sound. He emphasized the need for education and practice in becoming virtuous. It does not just happen, like growing taller or hairier. But the education is a matter of drawing out a 'latent' potential, at least in the best people (Aristotle is an elitist). The tradition that follows Aristotle is sometimes called the tradition of 'virtue ethics'. It heroically tries to squeeze together what is natural for people, a life lived according to reason, a happy life, and a virtuous life, seeing all these apparently different things as essentially one and the same. Its main device is the social nature of the self. Within society, the knave or villain cannot generally flourish, either in the eyes of others, or, ultimately, in his own eyes. The life of injustice is apt to be a life of care and insecurity. If someone prospers by thieving or cheating, his prosperity is likely to turn to ashes.

Perhaps this is likely, but it is not at all certain. We only need to think of the way that fraudsters flourish in the environment of the web to realize that it is a political achievement to make sure that departures from virtue bring ruin. Still, it is good to notice that for many purposes that may be enough. A general correlation between an agent's obvious lapses from virtue and her decline from flourishing is enough, for instance, for the purpose of the educator with the subject's interest at heart. We should educate people for whom we care into the habits that are most likely to benefit them, and on this account, these will be the paths of virtue. The educator will not countenance a habit of cheating or lying or taking opportunistic advantage of others, since these things generally diminish the agent's well-being. Generally speaking, people do well by doing good, or at least by avoiding doing bad.

Up to a point, no doubt. But it is surely wrong to think that an equation between living as we would wish and living virtuously is somehow written into things by nature. Insofar as it is approximately true, it is because it is written into things by culture. It is in the first place an *educational*, and also a *political* achievement, and one that needs constant attention. This is for at least three reasons. First, it takes education to instil into the subject the sense of respect and self-respect which will turn a profit made by losing his soul into a loss. A sufficiently bare-faced villain just won't care. Second, it takes a secure and stable political or social system to generate bad effects on the villain, such as loss due to discovery, or loss of reputation. When things are in flux, the villain will be able to cheat and move on. Third, it takes a culture or politics to properly identify a lapse from virtue in any case.

To see this last point we need only consider examples of oppressive societies. Suppose women systematically lack opportunities and resources that the men have. Men (and women) in such a society may not be conscious of anything wrong here. They have internalized the traditional values. Their conception of what it is for a woman to flourish will be that she is nicely subservient or obedient to the men. In such a world the man oppressing the woman has no bad conscience, and suffers no loss of respect from those he cares about—mainly other men. He can flourish, in his own eyes, and his friends' eyes, and even in the eyes of the women. The case would be even more obvious if we took behaviour towards people outside the community. Consider the wealthy white male who flourishes because of the economic and educational deprivations of people, including children, in the third world. It takes something more than a desire to flourish to motivate in him a serious concern for *them*. He is all too likely to measure his flourishing only against people like himself.

The modern Aristotelian, less inclined to discount inferiors and outsiders than Aristotle himself, can fight back. She can say that such cases need sustaining by rationalizations, and these rationalizations will mainly consist in lies the privileged tell themselves. And a life lived amidst lies, or in a fool's paradise, is not a flourishing life. So the ingredients are there to suggest that *real* flourishing or *true* human health implies justice. It implies removing the oppression, and living so that we can look other people, even outsiders, in the eye.

However, this need for rationalizations is itself not a given. Sometimes, as we go our careless ways, we do not even seem to need lies to sustain us. Our generation may flourish by consuming all the world's resources, and letting the future go hang. We do not tell ourselves a story according to which the generations to come are inferior to us and deserve to inherit a deadened world. Mostly we just don't think about it, and even if they admire movements such as Extinction Rebellion most people pay little more than lip service to their demands. Like their peers, Extinction Rebels want the heating left on, and seem to leave a lot of litter about.

Are we being 'unreasonable' as we discount or forget about dispossessed outsiders? We are certainly failing in benevolence, and we may be failing in justice (more on this below). But even if we concede much to the Aristotelian argument, we might remain pessimistic about its effect. Insofar as it works by 'pumping up' what is required for a life of reason or a life of *true* flourishing, we will find people perfectly ready to settle for a good fake. Better to buy the cheap running shoes and not to think too much about how they got made.

11. The categorical imperative

The second answer to Hume's challenge to the role of Reasons was given by Immanuel Kant. We can approach his views by thinking of a common gambit in practical discussion. When we try to stop people acting in some sneaky way, a good question is often: 'What if everybody did that?' The test is sometimes called a 'universalization' test. If the answer is that something would go especially wrong if everybody did that, then we are supposed to feel badly about doing it. Perhaps, for instance, we would be claiming an exemption from some rule of conduct for ourselves that we couldn't allow to people in general.

Kant picked up the universalization test and ran with it. In his hands it became not only a particular argument *within* ethics—a device, as it were, for making people think twice, or feel guilty—but the indispensable basis *for* ethics. It became the foundation stone for ethics, grounding ethics in reason alone. It gives us upper-case Reasons, even in the domain of practical choice and desire. He unveils the way this happens in his short masterpiece, *The Groundwork of the Metaphysics of Morals* of 1785, a work that has probably inspired more love and hatred, and more passionate commentary, than any other in the history of moral philosophy.

The universalization test can sound like a version of the Golden Rule: 'Do as you would be done by'—a rule sometimes claimed by Christianity as its own, but found in some form in almost every ethical tradition, including that of Confucius (551–479 BC). Kant denies that his idea is just that of the Golden Rule. It is supposed to have more meat. He points out, for example, that the golden rule can be misapplied. A criminal can throw it at a judge, asking him how he would like it if he were being sentenced.—Yet the sentence may be just for all that. A person in good circumstances may complacently agree that others should not benefit him, if he could be excused from benefiting them. He apparently abides by the Golden Rule. So something with more structure is needed.

Kant starts by distinguishing what he wants to talk about from what he calls talents of the mind, such as understanding, wit, or judgement, and from advantages of temperament, such as courage or perseverance or even benevolence. He also distinguishes it from gifts of fortune, happiness, and even admirable qualities such as moderation. None of these are 'good in themselves'. For all of them can be misused, or can be lamented. Even happiness is not admirable, if it is the happiness of a villain. Benevolence may lead us astray, letting other people enjoy what they have no right to enjoy, for example. And 'the very coolness of a scoundrel makes him not only far more dangerous but also immediately more abominable in our eyes than we would have taken him to be without it'.

The only thing good in itself, then, is a good will. Even if the agent with the good will is handicapped, 'by a special disfavour of destiny or by the niggardly endowment of stepmotherly nature', from actually doing much good in the world, still if he has a good will, it must 'shine like a jewel for its own sake'.

But what is a good will? Kant considers cases of people doing good things, things that might even be their duty, not, however, from a sense of duty, but from other inclinations, such as self-interest, or even benevolence, or a sense of vanity. A salient example is a shopkeeper who does not overcharge an inexperienced customer, but only because his self-interest is served by not doing so. Perhaps he calculates that the customer is more likely to return, or that his shop will profit from a good reputation. The shopkeeper behaves honestly enough, but not because he has the right feeling that he *ought* to do so. There is no jewel shining by itself here. This is not the good will in operation. So what is?

The shape of the answer becomes clear from such examples. The good will is one acting from a particular good motive. It is one acting out of a sense of law or duty. 'Duty is the necessity of an action from respect for law.' We are able to represent laws of action in ourselves, and a good will is one that acts in accordance with that representation. The core of morality, then, lies not in what we do, but in our motives in doing it: 'When moral worth is at issue, what counts is not actions, which one sees, but those inner principles of action that one does not see.'

This is all very well, we might say. Kant seems to be praising up the conscientious agent, or the agent of principle or righteousness or rectitude. This is a person who, once he thinks 'Such-and-such is a duty' is strong-minded or principled enough not to be deflected from doing it. This is in some respects an admirable psychology, although it is also one that can do a lot of harm, since people's consciences can be as perverted as anything else. One wonders why righteousness in this sense is exempt from the criticism levelled at benevolence or efficiency in action, that employed in the wrong way they can be a Bad Thing.

Some writers also remind us that in many of life's situations, rectitude is not what we want. We often want people to act out of love or gratitude, not out of duty. Good parents take their child to an entertainment because they enjoy the child's pleasure; a parent who takes the child out of a sense of duty is not quite the thing. A lover who kisses out of a sense of duty is due for the boot. But this is not a fundamental criticism of Kant. He can, and does, allow dimensions in which the good-hearted parent or lover or benefactor scores highly. It is just that these are not, for him, the *moral* dimension. Moral excellence is found only in the strength of the sense of duty.

There is a more fundamental difficulty. Kant's answer seems to demand that certain things got onto a list of duties *in the first place*. It is no good saying 'Act from a sense of duty!' if when asked the question 'And what is my duty?', the only reply is 'To act from a sense of duty!' We have to break out of the circle somewhere, and so far we do not know how. So how is it all going to get us nearer to the foundations Kant promises? His move is breathtaking, in both its speed and its result:

> But what kind of law can that be, the representation of which must determine the will, even without regard for the effect expected from it, in order for the will to be called good absolutely and without limitation? Since I have deprived the will of every impulse that could arise for it from obeying some law, nothing is left but the conformity of actions as such with universal law, which alone is to serve the will as its principle, that is, *I ought never to act except in such a way that I could also will that my maxim should become a universal law.*

This is the famous categorical imperative, or more accurately, the categorical imperative in its first form, the so-called Formula of

53

Universal Law. Later on Kant glosses it in other ways. One is 'Act as if the maxim of your action were to become by your will a *universal law of nature*' (the Formula of the Law of Nature). Another, possibly the most influential, is 'So act that you use humanity, whether in your own person or in the person of any other, always at the same time as an end, never merely as a means' (the Formula of Humanity). It is not at all clear that these different versions can be derived one from the other, but Kant regarded them as somehow equivalent.

The promise is that we have here both quite substantial moral principles, or versions of the one principle, and that these are principles that have been proved by reason alone. This last claim is hard to make good, but perhaps the idea goes like this.

As Hume illustrates, we might suppose that there are no Reasons in the area of ethics—just the desires or wills of particular persons, not necessarily shared or respected by anyone else. But Kant thinks that the very formal nature of the categorical imperative gives it a universal authority. You cannot flout it and defend your principle in doing so. If you do flout it, you declare yourself to be un-Reasonable. If this is right, we have the required foundation: ethics comes from Reasons alone.

The most persuasive examples of the categorical imperative doing some real work are cases where there is an institution whose existence depends on sufficient performance by a sufficient number of people. Suppose, as is plausible, that our ability to give and receive promises depends upon general compliance with the principle of keeping promises. Were we to break them sufficiently often, or were promise-breaking to become a 'law of nature', then there would be no such thing as promise-giving or promise-breaking, because no words could any longer have the required force. So, Kant considers somebody whose principle of action is 'Let me, when hard pressed, make a promise with the intention not to keep it.' Then, says Kant, I could will the lie, but I could *not* will the universal law to lie, for in accordance with such a law there would be no promises at all. It would be willing a kind of contradiction. So we have a Reason against the lying promise.

That's all very well, but consider a person who is indifferent to the whole business of giving and receiving promises. Why shouldn't he ignore any damage to the institution? After all, this would be a plausible diagnosis of many contemporary politicians. They just don't care about any long-term damage their lying ways cause. Of course, nice or benevolent or prudent persons wouldn't be so careless or complacent, but if Kant appeals to these virtues his difference from Hume and Smith vanishes. We only have a reason against giving the lying promise, not a Reason.

Kant descends somewhat from the abstract heights of the 'formula of universal law' version of the categorical imperative. He hymns the way we can distance ourselves from our mundane desires and wishes, and set ourselves to act as duty requires. This capacity itself gives us our fundamental title to respect and self-respect. It deserves respect wherever it is found, that is, within all rational agents.

This argument (or something like it: the texts are dense) takes Kant to the formula of humanity: 'So act that you use humanity, whether in your own person or in the person of any other, always at the same time as an end, never merely as a means.' It is not, of course, easy to see exactly what this involves, but the general idea of remembering to respect each other is clearly attractive, and perhaps more practicable than remembering to love each other. Whether we deserve respect purely because of our capacity to make laws to ourselves is a good deal less certain. Perhaps we deserve respect from each other insofar as we are like each other in a whole mass of ways.

Many people think Kant offers the best possible attempt to find Reasons, and therefore to justify ethics on the basis of reason alone. Since many people want such an attempt to succeed, and fear the result if it does not, there are major intellectual industries of trying to find ever more complicated interpretations of the attempt that make it work. It's a worthy ambition, but it is doubtful whether it does much to improve on the urbane views of Hume and Smith. After all, if we return to the complacent wealthy individual who cares little for the plight of others, it is unlikely that we will get much traction by suggesting that he is ignoring binding, inescapable, Reasons for being better. Like the lying politician, if his conscience is already slumbering it is unlikely to awaken because Kant tells him that as well as being unimaginative, callous, and selfish, he is also irrational.

12. The state of nature

If our capacity for ethical behaviour is not immediately given by our nature as human beings, nor by an inescapable birthright of reason, where does it come from? Perhaps it is a social construction? In the modern world one of the earliest and most influential attempts to answer the question this way was that of Thomas Hobbes (1588–1679). Hobbes imagined a pre-social world in which individuals bent on their own survival lived in competition for resources. Famously he described this as the war of all against all, 'No Arts; no Letters; no Society; and which is worst of all, continual Fear, and danger of violent death; And the life of man solitary, poor, nasty, brutish, and short.' How could people pull themselves out of this fearful state? Hobbes makes two moves. First he supposes that his agents can get together and contract into a common policy. And second he thinks that their common policy could or should be one of submitting to a sovereign, or in other words voluntarily handing a monopoly of power to one agent, who, it is then assumed, will hold the ring, using the monopoly so granted for the benefit of all. John Locke's comment on this second stage is well known, but good enough to repeat:

> As if when men, quitting the state of Nature, entered into society,
> they agreed that all of them but one should be under the restraint of

laws; but that he should still retain all the liberty of the state of Nature, increased with power, and made licentious by impunity. This is to think that men are so foolish that they take care to avoid what mischiefs may be done them by polecats or foxes, but are content, nay, think it safety, to be devoured by lions.

But philosophically the more interesting problems already arise at the first stage. How are Hobbesian agents supposed to enter into a contract or binding agreement? Hobbes saw the problem clearly enough:

> If a covenant be made...in the condition of mere nature, (which is a condition of war of every man against every man,) upon any reasonable suspicion it is void...for he that performeth first, has no assurance the other will perform after, because the bonds of words are too weak to bridle men's ambition, avarice, anger, and other passions...and therefore he which performeth first, does but betray himself to his enemy.

It takes a precondition of minimal trust for me to enter an agreement to lay down my arms on your say-so that you will also do so, or to do a job for you on your say-so that you will return the favour later, and this trust does not exist in the imagined state of nature.

If we postulate a state of nature like that of Hobbes, and a ruthlessly self-interested human animal, then apparently the problem of getting more than minimal social relations up and running is insoluble. The minimal social relations that might exist would be those of reciprocity, where I temporarily sacrifice some of my own interests, doing something for another, but only on the expectation that he does something at least equivalent for me. Even reciprocity however needs assurance. I am just a patsy if I spend my morning getting fleas out of your hide unless I can expect you to return the favour, and in Hobbes's world there is no way to give that assurance. Someone once quipped that a verbal

57

promise is not worth the paper it is written on. But in Hobbes's world, even written promises are not worth anything either.

Some writers have complained that Hobbes's problem is not, so far as we know, one that human beings ever had to face. There never was a state of nature, and we are not the egoistical monsters that Hobbes assumed. But we come to understand our concepts better if we can understand the way they might have developed from a previous state. This does not need to be a matter of providing an actual history with dated events and times. It can start with a type of state that we can imagine to have existed, and a plausible series of changes that would have ended up with us as we are.

From an evolutionary perspective the emergence of conventions of restraint and cooperation is a problem as long as we suppose that animals that sacrifice their own fitness for others must surely lose in the Darwinian struggle for reproductive success. So it is all very well saying that the human being is a social animal, but if biological theory appears to deny that any such animal can exist, we are still left with a problem.

The emergence of something better is usually modelled by means of simple games, of which the best known is the famous 'prisoner's dilemma'. In such a situation it is socially best if we come to some cooperative arrangement. But each of us can look after our own interests best by defecting from this arrangement. In the original story, a prosecutor has two suspects, Adam and Eve, who are charged with a crime. But he needs a confession. So he gives each of them, independently, a choice to confess or not. If you confess, he says to each, then if the other confesses too you will be convicted, and serve two years each. But if you confess and the other does not you will get off scot free, for having helped the court, although the other who does not confess will be convicted and hammered as a hard case, serving three years. But if the other does not confess either, you will each serve one year on the lesser charge of wasting police time. It is easy to verify that each prisoner has a decisive argument from self-interest for confessing: you do better by confessing *whatever the other does*. If the other confesses you had better do so as well, so serving two years instead of three and if the other sits tight you can confess and get off scot free. Yet if each follows this policy the social outcome is worst of all (four person-years in prison, when by each staying silent they could have accumulated only two person-years in prison; one each). It is as if instead of the invisible hand imagined by Adam Smith, whereby an atomistic society of self-interested individuals unintentionally improved the social world for everyone, there is an invisible boot whereby the same individuals unintentionally drive society towards the worst outcome.

Of course, the prisoners' situation is highly unusual. But many real life situations can be modelled as (multi-person) prisoners' dilemmas, in which self-interested reasoning will lead to a non-cooperative, worse, situation, yet the self-interested argument is good enough to tempt us. If there is a water shortage, the best social result is that we each restrain our usage. But if the others restrain their usage, my self-interest is better served by using as much water as I wish (one person's usage does not make much difference to the overall supply). Whilst if the others do not restrain their usage, my self-interest means that I had better not do so either: the water is going to run out anyhow, and I need to have watered my garden and taken my showers before it does so. It is similar with the temptation to fish to an unsustainable level, to go in for aggressive wage rises, to keep guns, and so on.

Other social problems are better mirrored by a closely related structure, the so-called assurance game. The classic example of this is the stag hunt, described by Jean-Jacques Rousseau. We have to join together to hunt a stag: perhaps we each need to stop one of the exits from the wood, and if one is left unstopped the stag will escape. If we do catch one then we will each share the result and that is best of all individually (unlike in the prisoners' dilemma, where confessing is individually better). Unfortunately each of us has a temptation to leave our post: there are hares about, and one can catch a hare all by oneself. Hares are good to eat: much better than nothing, even if not quite so good as a portion of stag. But now each of us needs assurance that nobody else will be tempted to chase a hare. If someone does, any of us who stand by our post ends up with nothing. Too great a risk, we might think, in which case we all chase hares, and end up with the second-best outcome all round. Too bad, but nice guys finish last, say the more ruthless beasts in the jungle. Cooperation is for losers. Greed is good. A landscape of trust and cooperation is always ready to be invaded by free-loaders who can exploit it for their own benefit, and these are the ones who will win out in the end. Or are they?

Fortunately, no. We need to imagine repeated interactions of these kinds and suppose that in the mix there are examples of cooperation, for instance in families and kin groups, or in groups that can only survive through cooperative endeavours, such as together driving dangerous predators off their prey in order to profit from the food this makes available. Then it would not be long before it began to be noticed that these are the people doing better. If success is measured by number of descendants, and we use the prisoners' dilemma arithmetic in reverse (so that more is better) then the cooperative people are set to outbreed the others. They might have four descendants after a generation, whereas a group of defectors only have two. And if the trait is inherited, either by a genetic modification or by culture and upbringing, then even when a defector meets a cooperator, and has three children, they in turn will be defectors, and again set to do worse. Over a period, nice guys finish first.

13. The emergence of norms

In short an adaptive mutation in a gene may benefit individuals because it enables them to cooperate in a group, and may spread because it does so. It has recently been discovered that even trees cooperate, feeding nutrients to needy neighbours so that the forest as a whole benefits from their solidarity. And if trees can do it, it should not be surprising that we can.

The upshot is that while no plan or agreement can release us from a war of all against all, practice in cooperation and observation of its benefits can wean us from it, over time and with repeated experience. The first writer to understand this well was, once more, David Hume who saw this way the emergence of such things as conventions, whereby we do something together, each acting only on the supposition others will do their part. This can happen without any prior thought or prior signalling. It can just be something we do. In Hume's own example, two men rowing a boat together fall into a coordination with each other. Eventually our conventions give us the whole wonderful social apparatus of property, money, language, law, and government. Hume describes the norms that make up these practices as norms of justice. When you default on a promise or an expected instance of cooperation you do an injustice to someone. He aptly writes that:

> The happiness and prosperity of mankind, arising from the social virtue of benevolence and its subdivisions, may be compared to a wall, built by many hands; which still rises by each stone, that is heaped upon it, and receives encrease proportional to the diligence and care of each workman. The same happiness, raised by the social virtue of justice and its subdivisions, may be compared to the building of a vault, where each individual stone would, of itself, fall to the ground; nor is the whole fabric supported but by the mutual assistance and combination of its corresponding parts.

It is only once these developments take place in society that we find that full flowering of what philosophers describe as 'normativity': the arrival of norms of expected behaviour, defection from which is a social transgression. Norms give us the 'musts' that infuse social life. They are the cement in the vault Hume talks about. Some may be quite trivial as when children agree that if they play hide-and-seek whoever is 'it' must cover their eyes and count to ten, or it is agreed that when we play chess the king must only move one square at a time. Such 'musts' are there for our convenience, for without them activities such as hide-and-seek or chess become impossible. But the same construction underlies more serious activities and serious institutions: not games like hide-and-seek but the serious scaffoldings of life, like language, money, law, and trust.

Being governed by rules and norms may seem a hindrance to self-interest. But that is far from the truth. Norms are in fact the indispensable servants of enlightened self-interest. The rules of language determining how we must speak or write are there since without them communication becomes impossible; the fact that other people must abstain from your property is there because without it security and safety evaporate, and so on. Rights, duties, and arguably the whole notion of treating people justly, according to their deserts, here swim into view.

The boast in the popular song 'I did it my way' is one of the most absurd and nauseating lies ever to gain currency. You did it by sheltering under a vast arch, or if we prefer it, sitting on the top of a vast pyramid, acting in ways made possible only by the cooperative activities of countless others and countless generations. You spoke their language, ate the food they discovered, profited from the inventions they made, travelled their roads, used their money, and sheltered under their laws.

Hume saw that the conditional nature of these activities—the fact that we perform them only on the condition that others play along—implies a kind of reciprocity. As already mentioned in section 4 it is an elaboration of the idea that if you scratch my back I shall scratch yours, elevated to be a fundamental building block of the institutions of society.

This raises a thorny question of justice for those who have, as it were, little or nothing to bring to the bargain. It need not be in our self-interest to bring them into the circle. Rather unappealingly Hume bites the bullet:

> Were there a species of creatures, intermingled with men, which, though rational, were possessed of such inferior strength, both of body and mind, that they were incapable of all resistance, and could never, upon the highest provocation, make us feel the effects of their resentment; the necessary consequence, I think, is, that we should be bound, by the laws of humanity, to give gentle usage to these creatures, but should not, properly speaking, lie under any restraint of justice with regard to them...

There is a whiff here of might being right, whereby issues of justice do not arise when one party has all the power over another. The weaker can only rely on the benevolence of the stronger party, which is likely to be a fairly unreliable matter. The problem was well known in classical times. The historian Thucydides relates a chilling dialogue in which the stronger Athenians try to compel the weaker Melians to their will, threatening them with destruction, and dismissing contemptuously any appeal to justice in their dealings, claiming instead that it is a law amongst both gods and men that 'the strong do what they can, and the weak suffer as they must'.

Interestingly enough the philosopher Nietzsche, usually thought of as an opponent of normal morality, later came (perhaps unwittingly) to Hume's rescue. He thought that once justice was elevated to an ideal it would, as it were, spread its glow over ever greater areas of human interaction:

> Since, in accordance with their intellectual habit, men have forgotten the original purpose of so-called just and fair actions, and especially because children have for millennia been trained to

admire and imitate such actions, it has gradually come to appear
that a just action is an unegoistic one: but it is on this appearance
that the high value accorded it depends; and this high value is,
moreover, continually increasing, as all valuations do: for
something highly valued is striven for, imitated, multiplied through
sacrifice, and grows as the worth of the toil and zeal expended by
each individual is added to the worth of the valued thing.—How
little moral would the world appear without forgetfulness! A poet
could say that God has placed forgetfulness as a doorkeeper on the
threshold of the temple of human dignity.

The suggestion is that any pride in our ability to care about justice
requires forgetting its egoistic basis in interactions in which we
exchange benefits with reciprocal partners, although it has spread
from there to embrace much wider circles of our interactions. As
beneficiaries of these centuries of change, good people—not all of
us, and unfortunately not many governments—naturally feel
uneasy about unfair dealings with weaker partners. We find it
natural to take them into the sphere of justice, and good for us.

If Nietzsche's suggestion seems a little speculative we might want
to compare it with this case. Most of us feel uncomfortable if we
hear that people are trashing our reputations. Rightly so since a
loss of reputation is dangerous; it may precede all kinds of loss
and difficulty. Enlightened self-interest demands concern about it.
But we would also be uncomfortable to know that future
generations will say nothing but bad things about us (as well they
might, given that we are busy squandering the world's resources).
Why, when we can't suffer a single jot from anything they may
say? The answer parallels Nietzsche's. We have internalized the
value of a clear reputation to a point beyond its original
connection with self-interest. Adam Smith's impartial spectator,
the man within the breast, can act as trustee for any complaints of
future generations, powerless to deal with us as they are. And this
is all that Nietzsche is suggesting about justice.

Hume and Smith, sociable 18th-century gentlemen, start with a picture of human beings as reasonably benevolent, self-interested, capable of foresight, interested in each others' sentiments, and willing to take up a common point of view with others. Hume especially refused to take sides over what he called the dignity or meanness of human nature, although this was a hot topic at the time. He thought his genealogy required only that there should be 'some particle of the dove, kneaded in our nature, alongside elements of the wolf and the serpent'. There is not much talk at the earliest stage of cooperation of duty, rights, obligations, or rules. But these all swim into view under the heading of justice. Once institutions such as promise-giving and promise-taking, or property or law, are in place then we have rules or 'normativity'. We begin to think in terms of things we must do, or things we may demand from others.

Things stop being just a question of sympathy or concern, which admit of graduations, but of who has *rights*, or what *justice* requires or what our *duty* is; it is a question of what is *permissible* and what is *wrong*. These are called 'deontological' notions, after the Greek *deontos*, meaning duty. They have a coercive edge. They take us beyond what we admire, or regret, or prefer, or even what we want other people to prefer. They take us to thoughts about what the rules or norms require. Some writers see these notions as introducing polar opposites to ideas of things we happen to want, such as happiness, security, or liberty. But by seeing normativity as a natural outgrowth of our attempts to achieve these things together, Hume and Smith soften the contrast. We cannot have the pleasures that tennis gives without the rules of tennis, the shelter of the laws without the rule of law, and we cannot have the pleasures society opens to us without the conventions that make society possible.

Part 3
Some ethical ideas

14. Desire and meaning

We have all heard the woeful refrain. The human world is a nothing but strife, disorder, fear, and instability. Life is wearisome, a burden. Its hopes are delusive, its enjoyments are hollow. Desire is infinite and restless; gratification brings no peace. *Carpe diem* (seize the day)—but you cannot seize the day, for it vanishes into the past as you try. Everything tumbles into the abyss, nothing is stable; palaces and empires crumble to dust, the universe will grow cold, and all will be forgotten in the end.

> Vanity of vanity, saith the preacher, vanity of vanities, all is vanity. What profit hath a man for all his labour which he taketh under the sun?

The dead, beyond it all, are to be envied. Death is a luxury. Best of all not to have been born, but once born, better quickly dead.

The peril here is what the philosopher George Berkeley (1685–1753) called the vice of abstraction, or 'the fine and subtle net of abstract ideas which has so miserably perplexed and entangled the minds of men'. It is much easier to lament the hollow nature and the inconsistencies of desire if we stay out of focus, keeping the terms of discussion wholly abstract. Thus, it sounds miserable if desire is transient and mutable and apt to give rise only to further dissatisfactions. But is it really something to mope about? Thinking concretely, suppose we desire a good dinner, and enjoy it. Should it poison the enjoyment to reflect that it is transient (we won't enjoy this dinner for ever), or that the desire for a good dinner is changeable (soon we won't feel hungry), or only temporarily satisfied (we will want dinner again tomorrow)? It is not as if things would be better if we always wanted a dinner, or if having got a dinner once we never wanted one again, or if the one dinner went on for a whole lifetime. None of those things seems remotely desirable, so why make a fuss about it not being like that?

We similarly abstract when we ask whether life, en bloc as a single lump, 'has a meaning', imagining, perhaps, some external witness to it, which may even be ourselves from beyond the grave, looking back. Perhaps the imagined witness has the whole of time and space in its gaze, and to such a witness nothing on a human scale will have meaning. Indeed, it is hard to imagine how it could be visible at all—there is an awful *lot* of space and time out there. Our life shrinks to nothingness, just an insignificant, infinitesimal speck in the whole.

Why should our insignificance within that imagined perspective weigh on us? It is better if instead of fretting over an imaginary view we put ourselves in the position of the witness and judge. Each of us can ask whether life has meaning to *me*, here and now. The answer then depends. Life is a stream of lived events within which there is often plenty of meaning—for ourselves, and those around us. The architect Le Corbusier said that God lies in the details, and the same is true of meaning in life to us, here, now. The smile of her child means the earth to her mother, the touch means bliss for the lover, the turn of the phrase means happiness for the writer. Meaning comes with absorption and enjoyment, the flow of details that matter to us. The aim then should be to ensure that our lives have as many meaningful events as possible. We must avoid moods in which everything goes leaden. Anyone suffering from such a mood might sulk at the edge of the carnival, like Hamlet seeing nothing but futility of the world, the skull beneath the skin. It is sad when we become like that, and probably we need a tonic more than an argument. The only good argument, in a famous phrase of David Hume, is that this is no way to make yourself useful or agreeable to yourself or others. Hamlet was particularly disagreeable, and duly came to a sticky end.

15. The greatest happiness of the greatest number

A formula most people have heard is that of the greatest happiness of the greatest number. Utilitarianism is the moral philosophy putting that at the centre of things. It concentrates upon general well-wishing or benevolence, or *solidarity* or identification with the pleasures and pains or welfare of people as a whole. This is the impartial measure of how well things are going in general. The good is identified with the greatest happiness of the greatest number, and the aim of action is to advance the good (this is known as the principle of utility). Utilitarianism is *consequentialist*, or in other words forward-looking. It looks to the effects or consequences of actions in order to assess them. In this it contrasts with deontological ethics. An action that might be thought wrong, or undutiful, or unjust, or a trespass against someone's rights, might apparently be whitewashed or justified by its consequences, if it can be shown to be necessary or even conducive to the general good. Utilitarianism fits better with a 'gradualist' approach to ethical issues. It deals with value: with things being good or bad, or better or worse, as the greatest happiness of the greatest number increases or diminishes.

Deontological notions of justice, rights, duties, invoke the words of law, as much as words of ethics. Utilitarianism by contrast gives us the language of social goods. A utilitarian, faced with the issue of abortion, would look at the social conditions leading people to want abortions in the first place. Asked about a law, a utilitarian

Ethics

would wonder what benefits and harms arise from the criminalizing of activities. The cast of mind is that of the engineer, not the judge.

John Stuart Mill writes as if he thought that he had some kind of proof of the principle of utility. He thought desiring a thing and finding it pleasant are one and the same. So each individual is concerned, always and solely, for things only insofar as they are pleasant to that individual. So it follows, somehow, that everyone in general is concerned for everyone's pleasure, or for the general happiness. This is one of those cases where the argument is so bad that it is almost unbelievable that Mill could have used it, and the jury is out on that. In any event the conclusion not only fails to follow, but actually seems to contradict the starting point. It would be like arguing that since each person ties just his or her own shoelaces, everyone ties everyone's shoelaces. But except in a world of just one person if each person ties just his or her own shoelaces, *nobody* ties everyone's shoelaces. Similarly if we each desire what is pleasant to ourselves, then nobody desires what is pleasant to others, *unless* the pleasure of others is somehow an equal object of pleasure to each of us. This would be a world of indiscriminate universal sympathy: a nice world, but not quite the world we live in. People typically desire that they themselves get an enjoyment more than they desire that someone else gets it.

Even without the dubious help of this argument, we can still appreciate the aim of maximizing the general happiness. This aim is forward-looking, impartial, and egalitarian: everyone counts for one, and nobody for more than one. It is an aim we want people to have. This recognition is very old: benevolence or *jen* is the supreme virtue of Confucianism. And in public affairs it has a very respectable pedigree. It is an old legal maxim that 'Salus populi suprema lex': the safety of the people is the supreme law. If safety includes freedom from quite a lot of evils, and if that safety in turn makes up welfare or happiness, then we are close to utilitarianism.

Any decent ethic would want to cry up some virtue of benevolence, or altruism, or solidarity with the aim of increasing welfare and diminishing misery for everyone. The question is whether this is the only measure, so that everything else, and in particular the deontological notions we have already met, is subordinate to this goal. We might fear that just as a lot of crimes are committed in the name of liberty, so they can be committed in the name of the common happiness. Suppose just a little bit more happiness is obtained by trampling on someone's rights. Do we have to approve of that? Is justice itself subordinate to the general good? Suppose it creates more happiness to give a benefit to Amy who does not deserve it, than to Bertha, who does?

It can sound repugnant to think that we should balance justice against consequences, even when the consequences are impartial and general, and measured in terms of the most sophisticated notion of happiness we can describe. Perhaps part of us wants to thrill to a rival slogan: 'Fiat justitia et ruant coeli'—let justice be done though the heavens fall.

We seem to have a stark opposition between two slogans: 'Fiat justitia...' versus 'Salus populi...' But we have already met Hume responding by taking the best from both thoughts. Rules, including rules of property, promise-keeping, and rules concerning rights in general, are justified by their impact on the general happiness. The law is justified by the safety of the people. But this does not mean that the rules or the laws must *themselves* be forward-looking, always contingent upon the benefits to be obtained on the occasion. The system is artificial. It has a utilitarian justification, but the application of the rules in particular cases does not. For Hume, as we have seen, the whole edifice of justice, rights, duties, and law is a social creation essential to the well-being of society. This solution has become known as 'indirect' utilitarianism.

For a parallel, consider the rules of a game. The game may be there for a purpose—say, to provide pleasure for the spectators and the players. But the rules of the game determine how it is conducted. The rules are not to be bent on occasion, if the referee supposes that more pleasure will accrue to the spectators or players by the cheat. If people know that this is likely to happen their whole attitude changes, and the game may become impossible. The inflexibility of the rules is one thing that makes the game possible. Similarly, says the indirect utilitarian, we can only gain the general happiness, and particularly components of it such as security, by implementing fairly inflexible rules. We give each other property rights, fixed laws that bring determinate and foreseeable justice, and we instil general dispositions to conduct that can be relied upon, whatever the circumstances.

Or perhaps we should say, almost whatever the circumstances. Hume also pointed out that when things are bad enough, rights that would otherwise stand firm give way: 'What governor of a town makes any scruples of burning the suburbs, when they facilitate the approaches of the enemy?' In a sufficient emergency, even quite basic civil liberties properly go to the wall. In a fire, for instance, to get the spectators out of the threatened stadium, a referee might properly give a false call to terminate the game. In a shipwreck I can take possession of a passing plank to save myself, even if it is not a plank I own. Rules are often designed for ordinary cases, and can stand in the way of acceptable outcomes when applied in cases that are not ordinary.

But emergencies are rare, and it requires judgement to know when one is upon us. Emergencies permit exceptions, but the old stabilities and certainties can be reborn as soon as the emergency is over. A governor who burned the suburbs in wartime does not forfeit his general standing as protector of the laws, whereas one who appropriates a house for his favourite nephew does. The one can still be trusted, whereas the other cannot.

In its indirect forms utilitarianism has one enormous advantage. It explains how to judge whether particular rights, or rules, or even virtues of conduct *get to be on the list* of rights, rules, or virtues. They are to be there because they serve the common good. Other philosophies, lacking such a sensible and down-to-earth answer, must either duck the question or struggle to find different answers.

16. Freedom

Another approach to what matters in living well is to consider what has to be avoided. It is much easier, to begin with, to agree on this list. We don't want to suffer from the domination of others, or powerlessness, lack of opportunity, lack of capability, ignorance. We don't want to suffer pain, disease, misery, failure, disdain, pity, dependency, disrespect, depression, and melancholy. Hell was always easier to draw than heaven.

The list is of much more use to political philosophy. If we try to sketch what is required of a social order, it is much easier to say what has to be avoided, than what has to be achieved. A political order cannot do everything: it cannot guarantee a life free from depression or disease or disappointment. But it can give freedom from violence, discrimination, arbitrary arrest, inhuman or degrading punishment, unfair trials, and other evils. It can guarantee that you have the protection of the laws if you speak your mind (on some things) or peacefully demonstrate (sometimes). In this view, the moral or political or social order sets the scene. It can't help what people make of the scene. Whether people can go on to achieve the life of *eudaimonia* is up to them. It is not the job of a moral philosophy, and more than that of a constitution or a government to make people happy, but only to set a stage within which they *can* be happy. The American Declaration of Independence talks of 'Life, liberty and the pursuit of happiness', not the achievement of happiness.

This conception of the role of the political order is characteristic of liberalism. It is often said that its eyes are fixed on 'negative liberty'—people are to be free *from* various evils. This is contrasted with a more goal-driven or idealistic politics in which the aim is to enable people to *do* various good things or to *become* or *be* something desirable—positive liberty. But this may not be the best way of putting things, since any full specification of a freedom is apt to specify both what you are free from and what you are free to do. A freedom 'from' arbitrary arrest, for instance, is a freedom *to do* everything except some circumscribed range of things counting as crimes, without being arrested. A freedom *to* assemble peacefully is a freedom *from* legal penalty attaching to peaceful assembly. A freedom *from* taxation is a freedom *to* spend everything you earn without giving any to the government.

Nevertheless the contrast reminds us of something distinctive of liberalism, and of more intrusive political systems that depart from it. The more intrusive systems, such as socialism, communism, or fascism, are driven by some thicker vision of what is good than sheer freedom from legal or political interventions. So, for instance, an egalitarian might find it necessary to compromise some freedom of economic activity in order to bring about the desired outcome of rough economic equality. Many governments will compromise freedom of peaceable association if they suspect that the function of the association is to exacerbate hatreds and tensions within the society. Hegel found true freedom only in fairly rigorously structured political association, leading to the liberal Russell's gibe that for Hegel freedom means freedom to obey the police.

It can sound as if this is a simple clash, for instance between those who prioritize liberty and those who prioritize something else, such as peace or equality. But the language of liberty and freedom is apt to be confusing in these areas. For the word 'freedom' is flexible enough to cover these goals as well: freedom of economic activity is compromised in order to bring about freedom from economic disadvantage; freedom of association is compromised in order to bring about freedom from tension and hatred. Almost any positive good can be *described* in terms of freedom from something. Health is freedom from disease; happiness is a life free from flaws and miseries; equality is freedom from advantage and disadvantage. The word is itself available to everyone, leading to the kind of result the Roman historian Gibbon drily remarked about the Emperor Augustus:

> Augustus was sensible that mankind is governed by names; nor was he deceived in his expectation, that the senate and people would submit to slavery, provided they were respectfully assured that they still enjoyed their ancient freedom.

Faced with this flexibility, the theorist will need to prioritize some freedoms and discount others. At its extreme we may get the view that only some particular kind of life makes for 'real freedom'. Real freedom might, for instance, be freedom from the bondage of desire, as in Buddhism and Stoicism. Or it might be a kind of self-realization or self-perfection only possible in a community of similarly self-realized individuals, pointing us towards a communitarian, socialist, or even communist ideal. To a laissez-faire capitalist it might be freedom from more than minimal necessary political and legal interference in the pursuit of profit. But the rhetoric of freedom will typically just disguise the merits or demerits of the political order being promoted.

Although freedom from various obvious evils is an easy goal to agree upon, it is no accident that the main traditions in moral philosophy also deal in the more positive concepts of happiness or *eudaimonia* or self-realization. For the absence of pains and miseries is, by itself, too grey and neutral to excite our ambition and admiration. Of course, it may be far more urgent, for many people much of the time, to remove the bad things than to worry much about which good things we would like to succeed them.

But we can't entirely do without a vision of what life would be like at its best.

17. Paternalism

The flexibility of the term 'freedom' undoubtedly plays a huge role in the rhetoric of political demands, particularly when the language of rights mingles with the language of freedom. 'We have a right to freedom from...' is not only a good way, but the best way to start a moral or political demand.

Freedom is a dangerous word, just because it is an inspirational one. The politics appropriate for societies of such individuals are above all democratic. The enemy here would be any elitism, or paternalism, supposing that some particular kinds of people, through superior reason or knowledge or wisdom, are best fitted to govern the rest, since they know people's interests (their *real* interests) better than the people themselves do. The elitist doctrine is that the freedom of the ignorant and those with no self-control is just frightening and useless *licence*. The most celebrated account of the elitist image is due to Plato's *Republic*. In the argument of that book, government should be in the hands of disinterested and selfless rulers or guardians who have been rigorously educated into wisdom. The mob has no right of self-determination. It is there to be governed; it is not to be allowed to find its own way of life or make its own mistakes.

We might disapprove of Plato and approve of democracy instead. But we may want to be a bit nervous of the sustaining myth associated with it. The modern emphasis on freedom is problematically associated with a particular self-image. This is the 'autonomous' or self-governing and self-driven individual. This individual has the right to make his or her own decisions. Interference or restraint is lack of respect, and everyone has a right to respect. For this individual the ultimate irrationality would be to alienate his freedom, for instance by joining a monastery that requires unquestioning obedience to a superior, or selling himself into slavery to another. Such an action would amount to a kind of suicide, a defeat of what makes each human being unique and equally valuable.

The self-image may be sustained by the Kantian thought that each individual has the same share of human reason, and an equal right to deploy this reason in the conduct of his or her own life. Yet the 'autonomous' individual, gloriously independent in his decision-making, can easily seem to be a fantasy. Any moderately sober reflection on human life and human societies suggests that we are creatures easily swayed, constantly infected by the opinions of others, lacking critical self-understanding, easily gripped by fantastical hopes and ambitions. Our capacity for self-government is spasmodic, and even while we preen ourselves on our critical and independent, free and rational, decisions we are the slaves of fashion and opinion and social and cultural forces of which we are ignorant. It would often be good, and no signal of disrespect to ourselves, if those who know better could rescue us from our worst follies.

Perhaps, then, a more realistic defence of the freedoms we want to protect avoids the fantasy of our rational freedom. A more realistic defence might just be glum about the possibility of Plato's elite. The old question from Juvenal's sixth Satire surfaces: who shall guard the guardians? Winston Churchill is supposed to have said that democracy is the worst system of government ever invented—except for all the others. Nobody can be trusted to have unlimited power over another, nor to govern in the interests of others. The elite are human too. The grim histories of anti-democratic politics stand as awful reminders of the dangers in Plato's aristocratic myth. Plato himself was glum about this in the real world. The guardians of his imagined world can only merit their role by an impracticable process of the most rigorous education. Plato does not provide any consoling myth at all for the jumped-up dictator who claims to know what is best for the people. Democratic politicians may be bad enough, but those sheltering behind a claim to know what is best for us are apt to be a lot worse.

Even in democracies, there are fascinating relics of the Platonic image of the guardians. The democratic United States has its process of 'judicial review', whereby the legal mandarins of the Supreme Court oversee and strike out democratically voted legislation. This is done in the name of the Constitution, this being a document to whose meaning the legal mandarins alone have privileged access. The parallel with a priesthood and its private access to the truth of the sacred texts is not hard to detect.

A dislike of elitism is also, typically, a dislike of paternalism: of being told what to do in our own interests. We naturally think of ourselves as the best judges of our own interests, and this will be part of our conception of ourselves as self-governing, rational individuals. On the other hand, in our hearts we know that sometimes it is better if our judgements are overridden, just as it is better for children that theirs are sometimes overridden. Safety legislation makes the worker wear a helmet or a safety harness, whether he wants to or not. In times of plague people may be required to wear face masks, again, whether they want to do so or not. Social security systems make people pay towards their support in old age, whether they want to or not. Most people accept seat-belt and motorcycle-helmet laws. These all represent restrictions on an agent's freedom made in the name of the agent's own good. But as we have seen, we can always reinvoke the word in explaining what the restrictions are good for. Social security gives us freedom from poverty in old age; safety laws give us freedom from death and destruction due to risks which we are apt to ignore.

As in the abortion debate, a little awareness of ethics will make us mistrustful of sound-bite-sized absolutes. Even sacred freedoms meet compromises, and take us into a world of balances. Free speech is sacred. Yet the law does not protect fraudulent speech, libellous speech, speech describing national secrets, speech inciting racial and other hatreds, speech inciting panic in crowded places, and so on. In return, though, we gain freedom from fraud, from misrepresentation of our characters and our doings, from enemy incursions, from civil unrest, from arbitrary risks of panic in crowds. For sure, there will always be difficult cases. There are websites giving people simple recipes for how to make bombs in their kitchens. Do we want a conception of free speech that protects those? What about the freedom of the rest of us to live our lives without a significant risk of being blown up by a crank? Many feminist philosophers argue that pornographic speech interferes with the freedom of women to live without being the objects of demeaning fantasy. This is an important freedom, for we have several times touched on the way in which the respect we have in the eyes of others is a component of happiness. But how does it stack up against the freedom of others, men and women, to communicate their fantasies, regrettable though those may be? It would be nice if there were a utilitarian calculus enabling us to measure the costs and benefits of permission and suppression, but it is hard to find one.

18. Rights and natural rights

At the beginning of section 17 we noticed how 'We have a right to freedom from . .' is not only a good way, but often the best way to start a moral or political demand.

Yet it also seems to suggest a recipe for boundless expansion: we can hear people demand without blushing a right to freedom from any disadvantage, unhappiness, offence, want, need, disappointment . . . It sounds desirable, until we reflect that the other side of a right in these contexts is a duty: a duty on the legal or political or economic order to protect them from disadvantage and the rest. And then we need to wonder whether it is just too costly, or not even possible, for us to labour under those duties.

The United Nations Declaration of Human Rights arguably falls into this trap sometimes. In addition to the civil rights we would presumably all wish to protect, it introduces a number of 'welfare rights'. It says, for example, that everyone has a right to realization of 'the economic social and cultural rights indispensable for his dignity and the free development of his personality'. This opens the door to just the inflation described: it is not too difficult to argue that dignity and free development require any of a flood of freedoms from this, that, or the other obstacle, right down to such ludicrous rights as freedom from failure to get a job through being unable to perform it.

The language of 'natural rights' has always been prey to this kind of criticism. For example, the Declaration of the Rights of Man and the Citizen of the French Revolution 'resolved to expound in a solemn declaration the natural, inalienable and sacred rights of man'. It maintained that in respect of their rights 'men are born and remain free and equal'. It announced that the final end of every political institution is the preservation of these rights: 'those of liberty, property, security and resistance to oppression'.

Yet these apparently harmless sentiments aroused a storm of philosophical doubt, partly fuelled by the violent anarchy of the French Revolution itself. Mainly, it is very unclear what a 'natural right' could mean. We can understand rights granted to citizens by law. We might even imagine these growing out of very primitive society in which people afford each other something akin to rights, by habits of forbearance. Suppose A forbears from interfering with B's space, or from using violence on B, or from soliciting sexual favours from B's partner. And suppose the society would be heavily down on A were he not to forbear. Then we might talk of a convention or even a contract of forbearance, and the beginning of a network of property rights and other social rights, as we already saw in section 13. B can appeal to the group to forbid or punish A's trespass, and by siding with B the others, in effect, confirm his right. But all that presupposes a society. What could exist by way of rights before or independently of a state of society? Would everyone have a right to everything? Or would nobody have a right to anything? The questions seem ludicrous.

But the language of natural rights need not be taken to raise them. It need not imply some pre-social state of nature in which, surprisingly, people nevertheless had rights of different kinds. It may be intended not as *description* of a never-never land, but as *prescription* of an order that any society should uphold. It will not then be to the point to say that the idea is unhistorical. Nor will it be to the point to say that actual society is not like this. People are not, for instance, born free—they are born into a civil order that will impose duties and obligations on them. They do not remain free in all kinds of respects, and they are not born equal and don't remain equal in all kinds of ways either. But the intention will be to criticize the existing order in the name of these ideals, or to work for an ideal that incorporates some notion of basic equality (equality before the law, for instance) and some central menu of freedoms.

Still, we might wonder about the reasons for the prescriptions. The word 'natural' in the phrase 'natural rights' might suggest a religious foundation. It would be as if God had posted on each of us at birth a small list of demands from others. If we do not find that idea appealing, then once more the word suggests some kind of Aristotelian story. Human beings will have a 'nature' that can only flourish in societies conforming to the declaration. These are the only societies in which they can 'realize' themselves or be 'truly' free. But that in turn might seem highly doubtful. We are pretty plastic and adaptive, and, as we have already seen, different conceptions of flourishing abound. Many think we flourish in the rich and liberal Western democracies of today. But some would say, for instance, that we can only really flourish in egalitarian societies where there are strict controls on the amount of property any one person or any one class can control. Others would say that we can only flourish under the umbrella of a strong social order, cemented by common adherence to a particular religious tradition.

We have seen that people's conception of their rights can be dangerously inflationary. There are other pragmatic or practical objections that have been raised. The language is abstract: how much property does a right to property give you? What duties does this right impose on others? How much does my right to life enable me to demand by way of care and resources, if those are necessary to keep me going? And we have already seen the infinitely flexible and treacherous ways in which the one-word concept of liberty can be stretched, so that a right to liberty can seem almost meaningless. One-word rights give no answer to the difficult questions.

The language is apt to be adversarial. It pits *me* against *them*, encouraging a sense of *my* right against others, *my* sense of just grievance when things don't go my way. It is not the language of genuine community; so much so that Bentham thought it was 'terrorist' language. Thus, we would not have very high expectations of a partnership in which each member is constantly checking whether his or her budget of rights has been infringed by the other. When pre-nuptial contracts specify a right to have half the washing up done, or the housework, or a right to shared child-caring duties, and sex no more than four and no less than three times a week, we should not be optimistic about the ensuing marriage. It is not that any of these things are bad—they may be desirable—but demanding them as a right implies that *me* has not been taken over by *we*. A hair-trigger sense of grievance is not a recipe for happy families. If *we* has not taken over from *me*, the attitudes needed for successful community are not in place. It is clear what Bentham would say about such a contract:

What has been the object, the perpetual and palpable object, of this declaration of pretended rights? To add as much force as possible to these passions, but already too strong—to burst the cords that hold them in,—to say to the selfish passions, there—everywhere—is your prey!—to the angry passions, there—everywhere—is your enemy. Such is the morality of this celebrated manifesto.

This was in fact the essence of Marx's criticism of 'bourgeois' or egoistic rights. For Marx, as for many social thinkers, the notion of a 'right' is centred in a morality that is atomistic and individualistic, concentrating on the demands of the single person, and forgetting the general good of the society within which the individual is necessarily situated.

Yet for other liberal thinkers, this is exactly what is good about it (and just look at the abysmal history of communist states where the notion of individual rights had little or no place). Rights, they argue, protect us against the encroachments of the society. Even in a democracy, a minority can need protection against the tyranny of the majority. Even if insisting on rights can be egoistic, and shrill, and sometimes insensitive, still, we need the notion. We need it to describe our dependencies and our need for protection from the predations of others, including the others in their collective or political guise. Even if it is foolish to dwell on an inflated list of rights on going into a marriage, still each partner does have rights against the other, and when they are badly infringed, redress and correction is required.

19. Birth and death

Throughout human history we have had only a few ways to control how many children get born, and who they are. We could control the gene pool, up to a point, by controlling who mates with whom. This could be done directly only by selection of a partner, or socially by arrangements of marriage and norms governing it. We could control how many get born, by abstinence, and perhaps by abortion. We can also control which of those that are born get to grow up, by infanticide, or selective standards of upbringing. This is far more important than generally realized. The Nobel prize-winning economist Amartya Sen has calculated that there are over 100 million 'missing women' worldwide. That is, statistics from not only the developed world but sub-Saharan Africa as well, give us that slightly more females exist than males. Given this, there are 100 million fewer living women than we should expect—44 million fewer in China and 37 million fewer in India alone. The difference is due to inequalities in medical care and sustenance, as well as deliberate infanticide, together making up the world's biggest issue of justice for women.

When we do any of these things we interfere with what would otherwise have happened. We might be said to interfere with nature. If 'interfering with nature' is, as some people suggest, 'playing God' and therefore wrong, then we have always played God. But that is not as bad as it seems. In that sense, we play God as well when we put up an umbrella, interfering with the natural tendency of rain to wet our heads. As humans, we are bound to attempt to cope with the natural world, making things happen that otherwise would not have happened, or preventing things from happening that otherwise would have happened. The charge of playing God has no *independent* force. That is, people only raise it when the interference in question upsets them. If we have already determined that some natural process must be allowed to run unchecked, or that interfering with it is too risky or too radical, we might use the words as a way of crystallizing our worry when people propose to interfere. When anaesthetics were discovered, some moralists complained that their use was impious. It was playing God. Genetically engineered crops generate the same heat today. The question is whether the upset and the worry are well founded. Most of us think it wasn't in the case of anaesthetics, and the jury is still out on genetically engineered crops.

As our technologies of control increase, so do the new questions about how to use them. The question of genetic control trails the hideous historical baggage of the 'eugenic' movement, with its assumptions of racial superiority and racial purity and of the worthlessness of handicapped lives. Knowledge of the genome introduces decisions and questions of control and power that are less apocalyptic, although to some people disturbing enough. If a test can show that a gene for some hereditary disease is present, should the test be done? Should it be grounds for an abortion? Should it be grounds for a compulsory abortion, for instance if the resulting child would need large resources in order to live? It is hard to answer such questions in the abstract, but what we can do is address the problem we very much have with us today, and that clearly underlies a lot of unease in this area: that of abortion itself.

The public debate is often conducted as if this is a black or white issue, a case of absolute right or wrong. You must be either pro-life or pro-choice. You either believe in the right to life of the not-yet-born or you believe in a woman's right to control her own body. A good first philosophical question to ask might be whether this black and white may be an illusion. It may be the result of a moral lens that imposes its black and white on a landscape of different shades of grey. After all, the biological facts of foetus development are gradual. The one-cell starting point or zygote is a different kettle of fish from the baby about to be born. But the complexity arrives gradually, hour by hour, day by day.

And then the reasons for which a woman might seek an abortion are *more or less* stringent and compelling. The poor, incompetent, frightened, raped 14-year-old is a different case from the socialite who would prefer to delay childbirth until after the skiing season, and a different case again is the woman wanting to abort a foetus because pre-natal testing has shown it is female.

If it were just a question of finding an appropriate attitude to abortion, we might go along with this gradualism. The woman seeking a late abortion because of the skiing would strike most of us as heartless in a rather disturbing way, just as a woman unperturbed by a late miscarriage would similarly strike us. She may, of course, turn round and say that it is none of our business, and after all there may be hidden fears or needs at work. We might not want to be too judgemental in any such cases, but we can still recognize that some reasons are more compelling than others. Perhaps for many people, especially in the liberal countries of Europe, a fairly tolerant gradualism is therefore the solution. But many cultures, including that of the United States, ratchet up the issue.

This happens when the question is politicized, becoming a matter of law. This is a step, because not all wrongdoings are criminal, and it is a political, and eventually an ethical, issue how far the law is allowed to intrude upon them. Indeed, one of the moral signatures of a society will be the extent to which the law allows liberty to do, feel, or think the wrong things. So even if we feel that there is at least a category of abortions that ought not to be performed, the question of criminalization remains open. They wouldn't be performed in an ideal world, but it is not the function of law to forbid and punish every departure from an ideal world. Even people who disapprove of alcohol may be aware that it was a very bad idea indeed to criminalize it.

It will seem natural to only one side of the debate to ratchet up the issue. It will seem natural only if we think that the issue is akin to an issue of murder. The foetus, on this view, is a person, and has a person's full rights and protections. Hence, it is a deontological issue and it is an issue for the law. But is this true?

A foetus is a potential person, certainly. But 'potential' is a dangerous word. A yellow flower is a sort of flower. But an acorn is a potential oak-tree without itself being an oak tree. My car is potential scrap, but it is not scrap, and its being potential scrap does not justify anybody in treating it as scrap.

Is the foetus not only a potential person but an actual person? What kind of question is that? A possibility is that in describing the foetus as a person, the word 'person' is itself functioning to imply a moral category, so by insisting that the foetus is a person the opponent of legal abortion is just repeating himself. Moral conclusions are frequently *presupposed* in just this way by the very terms in which the question is raised. A person, on this account, is just anything that ought to be treated as a person and afforded protection as a person. But then, whether a foetus is a person is exactly the question that is in doubt.

Suppose then we look for marks of increasing approximation to a person. We will find them at different stages. We might look out for the development of a functioning brain, or a capacity for 'distress' or for movement that at least resembles the behaviour which in persons expresses pain. The foetus is not, however, a subject with plans, intentions, fears, memories, or self-consciousness, each of which form part of our own adult personhood. These come later. And then it seems that there is no principled place to draw a line. The foetus, and the baby, starts as a cluster of cells, a zygote or blastocyst the size of a grain of rice, and then goes on to becoming *more and more* of a person. Nature is gradual, through and through.

Equally however, the T-shirt slogan of a woman's right to control her own body begs the question the other way: the ways in which we may control our bodies may well depend on what other persons are dependent upon them. So if the foetus is a person that right will be circumscribed. If a murderer is prowling around, my general right to talk is defeated by the fact that your life depends on my silence.

Rights are themselves tricky things, as we have already seen. In one of the most famous papers in this debate, the philosopher Judith Jarvis Thompson compared the situation of a pregnant mother to that of someone suddenly waking to find another person plugged into them and dependent on them for life-support. She argued that the dependent person's 'right to life' did not include a right to unlimited demands on other people, including here the demand that the supporter continues her support. The analogy introduces the important distinction between having a right to life, and having a right to the time or labour or energies of others that, as it happens, are necessary to support that life.

A bad argument to watch out for now has the form 'If there is no principled place to draw a line, then we must draw it *here*—at the very moment of conception'; or, if you stand on the woman's right to control her body, we should draw it only *there*—at the moment of birth. The idea is that anywhere else involves a 'slippery slope'. If you say that abortion is the killing of a person after five months, why not four months and three weeks? Four months and two weeks? Six months?

However 'slippery slope' reasoning needs to be resisted, not just here but everywhere. It is exemplified in the paradox of the bald man, known as the Sorites paradox. A man with no hairs on his head is bald. A man who is bald is never made not bald by the addition of just one hair. Hence (working upwards one hair at a time) a man with, say, 100,000 hairs on his head is bald. But that is just false! Such a man has a normal full head of hair. The paradox exercises logicians, but in moral and legal contexts it has no force. Consider the imposition of a speed limit. We choose a definite limit, say 30 miles per hour, and make it the law. We do not really believe that 29 miles per hour is always safe, and 31 is always not. But we would not listen to someone saying 'there is no principled place to draw a line, so we can't have a speed limit'. Nor would we listen to Sorites reasoning forcing the limit forever upwards, or forever downwards to zero. So, if we think the abortion issue does need moralizing and politicizing, nothing stops us from fixing a particular term of pregnancy beyond which abortion is generally prohibited. It won't have a firm metaphysical foundation, but perhaps, like the speed limit, it doesn't need one.

To return to the question of whether the foetus is a person consider the natural event of a natural miscarriage. Nature is not particularly sparing with these; they are quite common early in pregnancy, and may be very common in the first few days, when they are not necessarily noticed. Later on they can be very distressing, depending on the hopes that had been invested in the pregnancy. But they are not distressing in the same way as the death of a person. A parent who loses a child faces one of the worst experiences anyone can go through. There is someone to mourn, someone who had a life with hopes and dreams. But a prospective mother who suffers an early miscarriage does not have someone to mourn. She can mourn the loss of *what might have been*, and she can suffer for her own lost hopes and plans. But she has known no *actual* person who is lost (this may change late in pregnancy, when the child 'makes itself known'). For this reason, although she may deserve sympathy, she is not in the same category as the mother who loses a child. Hence too, even cultures that forbid abortion do not insist on full burial service for a dead foetus. The failure to get all the way to a birth in the family is not a death in the family.

Gradualism does not fit well with the deontological notions, which have an all-or-nothing flavour about them. Gradualism fits better with notions like things going more or less well, or people behaving more or less admirably, or more or less selfishly or callously. We might think it is better to work in terms of these notions. But when issues of life and death come into view, it is hard for many people to accept gradualist approaches.

In any case, what's so bad about death?

Epicurus had an argument that death should not be feared.

> Death is nothing to us, for that which is dissolved is without sensation; and that which lacks sensation is nothing to us.

The Stoics had reinforcements for this rather bare argument. One is to compare the state of non-existence after we die with our state of non-existence before we were born—and there was nothing to fear about that, was there? Another is to insist on the vanishing of time: death is just the same for one who died yesterday as for those who died centuries ago. This is the only way to make sense of 'eternity': death has no duration at all, for the subject. Andrew Marvell may have chivvied his reluctant mistress by reminding her that 'Yonder all before us lie | deserts of vast eternity' but these are not deserts anybody (ever) crosses. In other words, 'the state of being dead' is a misnomer. The fact that Kant is dead is not the fact that Kant is in some mysterious state, and going to be for a very, very long time. It is the fact that Kant no longer exists. Death is not the state *of* a person. It is 'nothing to us' because we no longer exist. It is not a kind of life: peaceful, reposed, reconciled, content, cold, lonely, dark, or anything else.

It is often felt that death is an enigma, perhaps the ultimate mystery. Why? Life is mysterious, insofar as it raises scientific questions. But then we have the life sciences to help us. The self-sustaining processes of life are reasonably understood. They are easily disrupted, and have finite lifetimes. When the time comes, they cease, and what was once alive, be it a leaf or a rose or a person, dies. There is no mystery about that, beyond unravelling the chemistry and biology of it.

Death can only be thought of as mysterious when we try to understand it by *imagining* it. And then we will be imagining 'what it will be like for *me*'. But death is like nothing for me, not because it is mysteriously unlike the things I have so far known, but because there is no me left.

Of course, all this is so if we deny ourselves the consolation of an afterlife. For many people, one of the attractions of the major religions is the promise of just such a life: a changed state of being, for better or worse. Ethics is one of the motivations to this belief. Life here is unjust or intolerable. So there must be a better one somewhere else. Or, it is intolerable that the unjust man meets happiness and success, and the just man meets misery and failure. So there must be another arena where justice is restored. Or, it is intolerable that some people, through no apparent fault of their own, are born to lives of want and misery. So, they must be being punished for some fault in a previous life. Such arguments sound suspiciously like wishful thinking rather than sound reasoning. Their form is 'things are in some respect intolerable here, so they must be better somewhere else'. But unless we are convinced of divine purpose, the truth may be that life is in these various respects intolerable here, and that's the end of it. And, as David Hume argued, even if we *are* convinced of divine purpose, there can only be one source of evidence of what it is. This must be what we find in the world around us. So if life here is unjust and intolerable, then the only defensible inference is that divinity intends a fair dose of things that are unjust and intolerable.

Many philosophers argue, and I agree, that belief in the afterlife involves an indefensible metaphysics: a false picture of how we as persons relate to our physical bodies. It imagines the soul as accidentally and only temporarily lodged in a body, like a person in a car. Whereas many philosophers think of the distinction between mind and body as much more subtle than this. They might say it is more like the distinction between the computer program and the machine on which it runs. There is a distinction, sure enough, but not one that gives you any licence to imagine the software running, but without any hardware at all.

If life after death is abandoned, the Stoics seem clearly right that death is not to be feared. Still, we need to disambiguate a little. Kant's death was an event, and it happened to Kant. It was the end of Kant's dying. In this sense, alas, when death comes we do exist, for we have to do the dying. It is only at the end of the process that there is no subject of the process. And we may reasonably fear the process. We all hope to go quickly, and quietly, and painlessly, and with dignity. We hope not to die in terror or pain. We like the fact that people are concerned to make dying easy. We laugh nervously at reports that doctors idiotically refuse pain-killers to the dying, on the grounds that they might become addicted.

However, as Woody Allen said, 'I wouldn't mind dying so much if it wasn't that I would be dead at the end of it.' Faced with a choice between dying, and undergoing a process just the same until the very last moment, when we recover, most of us would opt for the second. It would be bad, but not as bad as the other. So perhaps we don't really follow the Stoics in our hearts. It is not only the process of dying, but the subsequent annihilation that concerns us.

We fear annihilation more intensely the more we enjoy life. As we look forward we might hope for and prefer more time of good company, hot dinners, concerts, and sex, to only a brief final fling. If we suffer only the pseudo-dying, once we have recovered perhaps we shall get all that extra time. So of course that is preferable to the shorter span. We can mourn what we will never do. Equally, the death of a child is a more moving event than that of an adult, because of all that they never enjoyed and never did.

There is something mock-heroic about the stance that death is not an evil. If it is not an evil, then there seems to be a corollary, which is that there is nothing especially bad about killing; or, if there is, it is because it is bad for the relatives or friends. Yet the prohibition against killing has a central place in almost any morality. Even in societies which allow some killings—euthanasia, infanticide, execution of criminals, or prisoners of war, or political opponents—the boundaries are strict; places where they have broken down more or less entirely are places where society has dissolved.

Perhaps it is fairly easy to see why causing death should be the crime that it is. If a person is prepared to transgress against that rule, it seems that anything goes. But what then about desired death, such as suicide, assisted suicide, or euthanasia? Perhaps the most serious argument against these is that if they are a legitimate option, people will become attracted to them, or pressurized to accept them, by other people who stand to profit from their extinction. Hence, it is best to educate people to believe that these are just not an option, for otherwise those who are approaching death slowly will be put under pressure to speed things up. Myself, I cannot see this argument as very powerful. Relatives and providers can indeed pressurize the elderly and powerless to do all kinds of things they don't want to do. But the belief that those closest to you would be relieved if you died is a misfortune anyhow, whether or not there is the option of complying. The evil seems small and controllable, compared with many of the worst kinds of dying. As is often pointed out, in many countries, including England and the United States, you would be prosecuted for relieving a person from terminal suffering so bad that you would be prosecuted for *not* relieving an animal from it, by euthanasia. Why does the non-human animal deserve better than the human animal?

One issue that has much troubled moral philosophers here is the distinction between killing and letting die. Some codes of medical practice implement the old injunction, 'Thou shalt not kill, but need not strive | officiously to keep alive.' Opposition to euthanasia from within the medical profession often cites the 'volte-face' a doctor faces if, trained and accustomed to sustain life, he is suddenly asked to terminate it. On this reasoning, if a child is born terribly handicapped and needing outside support to live, or a person is certainly dying and their life is dependent on outside support, it would be wrong to administer a lethal injection, but all right to stand by and do nothing to support their life. This may salve some consciences, but it is very doubtful whether it ought to, since it often condemns the subject to a painful, lingering death, fighting for breath or dying of thirst, while those who could do something stand aside, withholding a merciful death. One wouldn't want it for oneself, or anybody one loves.

Part of the controversy here concerns whether withholding a necessity itself counts not just as letting die, but as killing. If I kidnap you and put you in my dungeon, that is not murder. But if I then withhold food, don't I murder you? In this case, I am responsible for you being dependent on me. But suppose you just happen to get into a situation where you are dependent upon me? Suppose by bad luck you just happen to be in my dungeon. Withholding food seems just as bad, or worse, than shooting you.

Ethical thought seems to need some distinction between what we permit to happen and what we actually cause. These cases only show how fragile the distinction can be. The distinction fits with a deontological cast of mind, insisting that it is what we *do* that raises questions of right and wrong, justice and duty. It is as if what we *allow* to happen, or what happens anyhow, without our intervention, isn't on our criminal record. But is it law rather than ethics that needs these cut-and-dried verdicts? Returning to the euthanasia issue, should we really admire the doctor waiting for nature to take its course, as opposed to the one prepared to bring down the curtain? Shouldn't it really be just a question of making sure that life, including the part of life that draws it to a close, goes better?

20. Decency, civility, and trust

Moralists have always feared the restless evil in the human heart. We do not have to believe in original sin to realize that there are strong forces at work that impede quite normal decencies and quite ordinary virtues. We can become depressed by the sheer amount of luck it takes to be good. Even when we live benevolent, admired lives according to the standards of our times, we can fear that had things been tougher we would have joined the fallen. If we are good, it may be because we were never tempted enough, or frightened enough or put in desperate enough need. We know that neither success nor suffering ennoble people. In such a mood, we can be overwhelmed just by the relentless human capacity for making life horrible for others. But the right reaction is not to succumb to the mood, but to reflect that the cure lies in our own hands.

A thread running through this book has been the way in which our abilities to coordinate with each other, respecting property, making and keeping promises, obeying the rules, make up the very fabric of society. Without these umbrellas the descent into the war of all against all would be frighteningly swift. Yet in countless ways, large and small, the trustworthiness of people can be fragile. When there is nothing much at stake we expect each other to be truthful and reasonably diligent. So, if we ask a stranger for the time, it is likely that they will take sufficient care over the answer (look at their watch, for example) and tell us the truth. But we teach children to be careful. When motivations creep in, such confidence quickly diminishes. Hence we doubt the word of salesmen, advertisers, anonymous sources, and governments. Trust is more secure when we have ongoing, repeated interactions with a small number of relatively permanent friends or neighbours. It is much less secure when people's identities are obscured, or transactions are one off, or it has been made impossible to mobilize social sanctions against the transgressors.

In the age of digital media this threat has ballooned. Fake reviews, fake goods, fake medicines, fake cures, fake descriptions of all kinds swamp the digital world. The torrents of bile and misinformation that pollute the web are often enough fraudulent and malevolent in their origin, but a major role in their dissemination is played by human weakness rather than actual intention to harm others. So, for example, the dangerous and foolish 'anti-vax' movement spreads carelessly rather than from ill-will. The completely false guess that there might be a causal connection between the measles, mumps, and rubella (MMR) vaccine and autism in children seized some people's imaginations, became believed and then tweeted and re-tweeted, and so took in ever more people. The dreadful thing, confirmed in many examples, is that once such a falsehood takes hold, trustworthy reliable evidence that there is in fact no causal connection of this kind becomes impotent against it. Inflamed and fearful parents themselves become immunized against understanding the absence of evidence and the real dangers that threaten their children and those of others when the diseases, against which they would once have been protected, emerge again. It is as if they simply cannot hear the authoritative voice of careful evidence-based scientific research. Worse than that, such evidence merely makes people 'double down', becoming ever more shrill in vilifying the science and ever more protective of their own illusions. Other examples include the denial of human involvement in climate change, and of course the proliferation of conspiracy theories of all kinds.

'Confirmation bias' is our propensity to accept and value anything that accords with our opinions and to dismiss and belittle whatever does not. This is a mechanism that insulates people from the truth, eventually rendering them immune to it. Philosophers and social scientists have puzzled over its prevalence, since in simple situations this propensity would be the reverse of an adaptation, and we might expect evolutionary pressures to eradicate it. In a primitive scenario if you think as you wake up that a route is safe, or that some berry is good to eat, you would be very unwise to dismiss evidence that it is not, or to double down on your original view in the face of such evidence. People inclined that way would leave fewer descendants than others. Contrary to popular belief, even ostriches do not bury their heads in the sand when danger threatens, which is just as well for them. So how does it arise that such propensities are so common?

The answer to this conundrum is that we are not like this across the board. Animals learn what to eat and what to avoid, and so by and large do we. But there are other cases in human life where other concerns bubble up. Some beliefs are pleasant, and others uncomfortable. Some are popular, at least in a circle we care about, and others are not. It is often more important to us to be part of the group, to play along with others, to be popular or admired, than it is to be orientated towards the truth.

There are many incentives whereby people become motivated to pass on things that are as likely, or indeed much more likely, to be false than not. Just the pleasure of having an interesting story to relate may be enough. We may wish the falsehood were true, and then fall into first pretending, and then gradually coming to believe that it is. It may be simply too uncomfortable to face up to the truth. And once we have given our word, it is socially very difficult to row back on it. So we double down, emphasizing our real, sacred, personal commitment to what might previously have been little more than a whim. We manufacture a kind of immunity to criticism and evidence in order to protect our self-esteem or pride. So people separate into tribes, or silos or bubbles where only voices like their own can be heard. Criticism is not invited. And circles become closed.

The first defence against fake news is the existence of trustworthy sources of information. This is why governments of all kinds have an uneasy relationship with the institutions that have earned trust over many years, and one of the first things any dictatorship does is to suppress the free press. Even in democracies the same can happen. The BBC for instance cannot be trusted by a government to slavishly repeat whatever lies or false promises the government would like to disseminate, and as I write this the triumphalist British government is bent on castrating it. We expect such censorship from dictators, but President Trump's campaigns against the quality press in the USA give even democratic governments around the world a model to follow.

The second major defence against fake news lies in our own hands. We do not have to be exceptionally pious or exceptionally virtuous to dislike spitting in the street, littering, and fly-tipping. We recognize their anti-social effects and wrinkle our noses when we come across them. It is not asking too much to expect an upbringing to teach children to share this aversion. I think we ought to put carelessness with the truth and the propensities that encourage it in the same category. Spreading misinformation is like spreading litter. It pollutes the social world just as effectively. Indeed insofar as it contributes to a general slovenliness of thought it is far more dangerous and more disastrous.

An education designed to minimize these unfortunate traits might have many prongs. One would be teaching the value of open and respectful debate. Children need to learn when opposite opinions deserve respect, and how to muster arguments both for and against things they may wish to hold. They also need to understand something of what makes one opinion worth more than another. Everyone knows that an opinion about the time is worth more if you have looked at your watch or phone and that an opinion about what is in the parcel is better grounded once you have opened it and looked. Often enough the aggressive question 'Who's to say?' can get a satisfactory answer: those who have investigated, calmly, without prejudice or bias, deploying knowledge and care. Children need to understand that science is basically an extension of these homely procedures. Where they have not given an answer, the method is to try again, not to plump for one dogma or another. Perhaps nothing will ever stop the madness of crowds, or turkeys voting for Christmas. But at least we can try.

For reasons that I have tried to bring out, ethics colours the whole of human life, from birth to death. It colours the whole of any society at any time, even although over time the particular shades it takes can change. If we are optimistic enough we might suppose, with Martin Luther King, that 'the arc of the moral universe is long, but it points towards justice'. If we are less optimistic we might see no such direction. But whichever way we incline, we have to recognize that we are all, in however small a way, implicated. If our ethics go badly, it is because we ourselves do.

References

Introduction

In G. W. F. Hegel, *The Phenomenology of Spirit* the interplay mentioned here is heavily dramatized as the so-called 'master–slave' dialectic, in section B, part A, pp. 111–19. The essential point is that if you don't recognize the value of others, their recognition of your value will in turn be meaningless to you. The point is more elegantly made in Groucho Marx's 'I wouldn't want to belong to any club that would have me as a member.' A more serious treatment is Charles Taylor, *Sources of the Self*.

Throughout the book, when I want to highlight a thought that separates insiders from outsiders, I shall use italics—it is the contrast between *us* and *them*. But I want the italic also to play something of a distancing role. For in many contexts to put the issue in terms of an 'us' and a 'them' is itself problematic. It suggests divisions into tribes or bubbles, and it suggests that each side is somehow monolithic, thereby fudging differences within groups. We almost always need to be sceptical about each implication.

Part 1: Seven threats to thinking about ethics

The most sustained philosophical campaign against the moral tone of Christianity was waged by Friedrich Nietzsche. See, for instance, *The AntiChrist* (1888). If we want a less philosophical version of the same kind of complaint, Robert Burns's poem 'Holy Willie's Prayer' is a marvellous dissection of the low-church, Presbyterian association of holiness with servility, self-satisfaction, and vindictiveness.

'The blessed and immortal nature...' Epicurus, 'Principal Doctrines', §1. *Epicurus: The Extant Remains*, p. 95.

'Everything goes to make me certain...', *The Histories*, 3. 38. P. 185.

'These homely methods...'. I call these methods homely, but they are also part of the foundations of scientific method. According to Mill's authoritative account, if you want to find whether one thing is responsible for another, you try varying the circumstances, and see if you can separate them. If you can the claim to unique causal responsibility fails. This is the method employed here. For more refined statements, see J. S. Mill, *A System of Logic*, Bk III, ch. 8, 'Of the Four Methods of Experimental Inquiry'.

Adam Smith's poor opinion of the motives that fuel consumers is often forgotten by apostles of free markets who like to flourish his name. See *The Theory of Moral Sentiments*, I, iii, 2, 1, p. 50. The idea can also be traced back to the 'wisdom' tradition including biblical works such as *Ecclesiastes*.

Dawkins himself invented a term for ideas which, as we say, 'have a life of their own'. He calls them memes. The selfish gene/selfish person meme is a particularly virulent one, in spite of being disowned by its parent.

'As Darwin himself saw...'. Darwin put it: 'When two tribes of primeval man, living in the same country, came into competition, if...the one tribe included a great number of courageous, sympathetic and faithful members, who were always ready to warn each other of danger, to aid and defend each other, this tribe would succeed better and conquer the other.' *The Descent of Man*, ch. 5.

However, a large chunk of Christian energy went into showing that sexual desire was itself voluntary, and hence a proper subject for guilt. See Michel Foucault, 'The Battle for Chastity', in *Essential Works of Foucault, 1954–84*, volume 1.

'Said in a lofty, disdainful tone...', Immanuel Kant, 'On the common saying: That may be correct in theory, but it is of no use in practice', *Practical Philosophy*, p. 280.

Part 2: Foundations

John Locke, 'The idea of a supreme Being', *An Essay Concerning Understanding*, IV, iii, 18.

David Hume, 'Tis not contrary...', *Treatise*, II, iii, 3.

David Hume, 'Reason is and ought to be…', *Treatise*, II, iii, 3.

David Hume, 'Besides discretion…' *Enquiry Concerning the Principles of Morals*, sec. 6, §21.

Immanuel Kant, 'The very coolness of a scoundrel…' This and the subsequent quotations are from *The Groundwork of the Metaphysics of Morals*.

Thomas Hobbes, 'No Arts, no Letters…' *Leviathan* XIII.

'As if when men…' John Locke, *Second Treatise of Civil Government*, ch. VII, sec. 93.

'If a covenant be made', Thomas Hobbes, *Leviathan* XIV.

A lot of political science, based on so-called 'rational actor' theory, would predict that events such as tipping the restaurant staff whom you will never meet again wouldn't happen. It would also predict that people don't vote, since the typical cost of voting in time and effort exceeds the expectation of gain from doing so. This is because the probability of your one vote making the difference is vanishingly small. Fortunately people do not generally behave as the theory would predict.

David Hume, 'The happiness and prosperity…' *Enquiry Concerning the Principles of Morals,* Appendix 3 §5.

Nietzsche, 'Since, in accordance…' *Human All too Human*, § 92.

Part 3: Some ethical ideas

'Vanity of vanity…' Ecclesiastes 1: 2–3.

George Berkeley, 'The fine and subtle net…' Introduction to *The Principles of Human Knowledge*, §7.

David Hume, 'What governor of a town…' *Essays Moral Political and Literary,* Part II, Essay xiii, 'Of Passive Obedience'.

Edward Gibbon, 'Augustus was sensible…' *Decline and Fall of the Roman Empire*, ch. 3.

Jeremy Bentham, 'What has been the object…' *Anarchical Fallacies*, quoted in Waldron, *Nonsense upon Stilts*, p. 44.

'Death is nothing to us…' *Epicurus*, 'Principal Doctrines', II, p. 95.

'Yonder all before us…' Andrew Marvell, 'To His Coy Mistress'.

Further reading

Part 1: Seven threats to thinking about ethics

Doubts about ethics itself are voiced in Nietzsche, *Beyond Good and Evil*, and many other works. See also John Mackie, *Ethics, Inventing Right and Wrong*, Bernard Williams, *Ethics and the Limits of Philosophy*, and Alasdair MacIntyre, *After Virtue*. Relativism is treated in Harman and Thompson, *Relativism and Moral Objectivity*, or David Wong, *Moral Relativity*. The theme of multiculturalism and universal ethics is treated in many papers in Martha Nussbaum and Jonathan Glover (eds), *Women, Culture, and Development*. The demandingness of ethics is uncomfortably visible in works such as Peter Unger, *Living High and Letting Die* or Shelly Kagan, *The Limits of Morality*. In fiction, works such as William Golding, *The Lord of the Flies*, or A. S. Byatt, *Babeltower* give lurid examples of moral breakdown in groups isolated from a culture.

Part 2: Foundations

On Kant's approach to ethics, see Thomas Hill, *Dignity and Practical Reason in Kant's Moral Theory*. For Aristotelianism and virtue ethics, see Alasdair MacIntyre, *After Virtue*, or more positively, Rosalind Hursthouse, *On Virtue Ethics*. On Contractarianism, see Brian Skyrms, *The Evolution of the Social Contract*, David Gauthier, *Ethics by Agreement*, or T. M. Scanlon, *What We Owe to Each Other*. An excellent collection of papers on the foundations of ethics is *Ethical Theory*, ed. LaFollette.

Part 3: Some ethical ideas

On missing women, see Amartya Sen, 'Women's Survival as a Development Problem', *Bulletin of the American Academy of Arts and Sciences*, 43, also 'Missing Women', *British Medical Journal*, 304, 1992. On the moral problem of abortions, see Lloyd Steffen (ed.), *Abortion: A Reader*. For more on the death wish, see Sigmund Freud, *Civilization and its Discontents*, and many other writings. For attitudes to death, see Thomas Nagel, *Mortal Questions*, or Jay Rosenberg, *Thinking Clearly about Death*. For a history of the subject, see Jonathan Dollimore, *Death, Desire and Loss*. On different conceptions of happiness, see Julia Annas, *The Morality of Happiness*. The classic statement of utilitarianism is John Stuart Mill, *Utilitarianism*. For 'indirect' utilitarianism, see R. M. Hare, *Moral Thinking: Its Method, Levels, and Point*. For a fascinating history of 'natural rights' see Jeremy Waldron's *Nonsense upon Stilts: Bentham, Burke and Marx on the Rights of Man*.

Index

A

abortion 37, 77
Allen, W. 91
Aristotle 47–9
autonomy 74–5

B

Bentham, J. 81
Berkeley, G. 66
biblical ethics 8–9
bubbles 96
Butler, J. 23–4
Burns, R. 45

C

Cambyses 14–15
categorical imperative 53–5
confirmation bias 95
Confucius 51
consequentialism 68
contracts 56–7, 79

D

Dawkins, R. 29
death 88–93

decency 47, 70, 93
Declaration
    of Human Rights 17
    of Independence 72
    of the Rights of Man 79–81
deontology 65–70, 85–93
dirty hands 35
Dostoevsky, F. 8

E

egoism 25, 58, 64, 82
Epicurus 11, 88
erotic desire 27
eudaimonia 72
euthanasia 91–3
Euthyphro dilemma 10
evolutionary theory 25–30, 58

F

fake news 96
feminist criticism 36, 78
flexibility 31–2
Foucault, M. 37
France, A. 37
freedom 69–80
Freud, S. 22
function, biological 13, 26–31

G

Gibbon, E. 74
God, death of 7–13
golden rule 51

H

happiness 51, 61, 68–71
Hegel, G. W. F. 1, 73
Hemingway, E. 39
Herodotus 14–15
Hobbes, T. 56–8
Hume, D. 42–54, 63–70, 90
Hutcheson, F. 42

I

infanticide 82–3

J

Jesus Christ 8–9
judicial review 77
justice 17, 34, 48–50, 61–8, 83, 98
Juvenal 76

K

Kant, I. 11, 32–5, 50–6, 76
King, M. L. 97

L

liberalism 17
Locke, J. 41–2, 56

M

Marvell, A. 89
Marx, G. 99
Marx, K. 13, 21, 82
Mill, J. S. 69
miscarriages 84, 88

missing women 83
Monty Python 13

N

natural rights 80
Nietzsche, F. 22, 37, 38, 63–4
norms 60–2

P

paternalism 75–8
personhood 86
Plato 2, 10–12, 75–7
pleasure 28, 53, 65, 66–71
pollution 97
pornography 78
prisoners' dilemma 58–9

R

reasons for action 19, 40–6, 50–6
reciprocal altruism 27, 57, 62, 64
relativism 13–19
respect 52, 55, 75, 97
rights see natural rights,
    Declaration(s) of rights
Rousseau, J. J. 59
Russell, B. 73

S

self-respect 49
Sen, A. 83
sexual desire 27, 30
sexual selection 28–9
Shaftesbury, 3rd Earl of 42
slippery slopes 87
Smith, A. 23, 44–6, 55–6, 64–5
Sorites paradox 87
stag hunt 59–60
state-of-nature see Hobbes, T.
Stoppard, T. 15
subjectivism 19
symbiosis 30

Ethics

T

Thucydides 63

U

universalization 50–1
utilitarianism 68–72

V

Veblen, T. 22–3
virtue 48–9, 55, 61, 69–72

W

Williams, B. 11, 47

CHRISTIAN ETHICS
A Very Short Introduction
D. Stephen Long

This *Very Short Introduction* to Christian ethics introduces the topic by examining its sources and historical basis. D. Stephen Long presents a discussion of the relationship between Christian ethics, modern, and postmodern ethics, and explores practical issues including sex, money, and power. Long recognises the inherent difficulties in bringing together 'Christian' and 'ethics' but argues that this is an important task for both the Christian faith and for ethics. Arguing that Christian ethics are not a precise science, but the cultivation of practical wisdom from a range of sources, Long also discusses some of the failures of the Christian tradition, including the crusades, the conquest, slavery, inquisitions, and the Galileo affair.

GERMAN
PHILOSOPHY
A Very Short Introduction
Andrew Bowie

German Philosophy: A Very Short Introduction discusses the
idea that German philosophy forms one of the most revealing
responses to the problems of 'modernity'. The rise of the modern
natural sciences and the related decline of religion raises a
series of questions, which recur throughout German philosophy,
concerning the relationships between knowledge and faith,
reason and emotion, and scientific, ethical, and artistic ways
of seeing the world. There are also many significant philosophers
who are generally neglected in most existing English-language
treatments of German philosophy, which tend to concentrate
on the canonical figures. This *Very Short Introduction* will include
reference to these thinkers and suggests how they can be
used to question more familiar German philosophical thought.

www.oup.com/vsi

HUMAN RIGHTS
A Very Short Introduction
Andrew Clapham

An appeal to human rights in the face of injustice can be a heartfelt and morally justified demand for some, while for others it remains merely an empty slogan. Taking an international perspective and focusing on highly topical issues such as torture, arbitrary detention, privacy, health and discrimination, this *Very Short Introduction* will help readers to understand for themselves the controversies and complexities behind this vitally relevant issue. Looking at the philosophical justification for rights, the historical origins of human rights and how they are formed in law, Andrew Clapham explains what our human rights actually are, what they might be, and where the human rights movement is heading.

www.oup.com/vsi